Building faith in the
Christadelphian community.

TIDINGS
Volume 87, Number 3 / March, 2024

IN THIS ISSUE

Introduction—The High Calling, **Dave Jennings** 2
Editorial—Deserters, **Dave Jennings** 4
Life Application—Deborah and Jael: Leading by Example as Servants,
      Sophie Robinson 9
Special Section—170 Years of Preaching in North America,
      Peter Hemingray 16
      —One Brother's Story, **Larry Sherfield** 24
Exhortation and Consolation—The White Space, **Jim Sullivan** 27
      —People Who Knew Jesus (5), **Rick Hill** 32
      —Hand in Hand, **Patricia Ferguson** 34
Bible Studies—Showing Faith, Reliance and Humility, **Tim Jennings** 36
      —Words I Hope I Never Hear Again (7), **David Levin** 42
First Principles—The Devil and Satan: An Old Testament Perspective,
      Richard Morgan 46
Bible Studies—Hamilton, Greenaway Ecclesia Centennial,
      Marilyne Creer 53
Letters to the Editor 56
Preaching and Teaching—Costa Rican Bible School, **David Collister** 58
      —Christadelphian Video Review, **Art Courtonel** 61
Thoughts on the Way—Public Prayer, **George Booker** 66

It is with deep gratitude that we have witnessed the hand of the LORD God leading thousands of men and women to a knowledge of the truth in distant lands. It is an assurance that the gospel is as alive as ever, bolstering the faith of those of us who live in regions where growth is more incremental or where our membership is in decline.

Today, well over half of our brothers and sisters do not speak English. These represent underserved members of our community, and we believe there is a significant need to provide edifying content for them. We are very excited to introduce a new multi-language magazine named *The High Calling*. This online-only publication is a collaboration between *The Tidings*, *The Christadelphian*, and *Glad Tidings* magazines, with the editorial responsibility being that of *The Christadelphian* and *Tidings* magazines.

Each month, we will select articles from the three magazines, translate them into other languages and make them available for free via flipbook technology. Brothers and sisters can both read and listen to text and recordings of these articles in their own language.

The first phase of *The High Calling* is in Persian Farsi. You can view the first edition by visiting thehighcalling.net. From the pilot testing that began last September, we have been thankful to receive some valuable feedback from our Farsi readers.

I have lived in Turkey for more than eight years, and I know the Persian Christadelphian community, which has more than 270 members. In Turkey, we don't have many sources to read in Farsi for exhortations or articles. We are blessed with this tool now, and on behalf of the Persian community, I am grateful for this. May God help you in your path to keep this magazine active! *Reza, Turkey*

As a Farsi-speaking mother, it was hard to find and read an article. Now, I can select and play any articles from this digital magazine; it even works when my phone is locked. Also, my five-year-old daughter likes to listen, and it will help her language skills and spiritual learning. Thank you! *Sanaz, Irvine, CA*

With this translated magazine and audio version, I am sure so many of our brothers and sisters could benefit from it and have access to articles that they couldn't understand before. *Mahan, Lake Forest, CA*

God willing, we plan to launch soon in other languages, including French, Portuguese, and Swahili. These are all important languages for our African brothers and sisters. We plan to include additional languages in 2025 and hope to work closely with the regional Bible Mission groups in this endeavor.

The spread of the gospel in the first century involved each person being able to hear and understand the words of truth in their own tongue (Acts 2:8).

While we don't have access to that Spirit gift today, we acknowledge that our goal must be to invest in the translated word. May God bless this work.

Dave Jennings,
Editor,
The Christadelphian Tidings

Mark Vincent,
Editor,
The Christadelphian

Chris Parkin,
Editor,
Glad Tidings

The High Calling Reach in 2024, Lord Willing
Farsi
Iran, Turkey, United Kingdom, North America
French
African Countries: Benin, Burkina Faso, Burundi, Cameroon, Central African Republic, Chad, Comoros, Cote d'Ivoire, Democratic Republic of Congo, Djibouti, Equatorial Guinea, Gabon, Guinea, Madagascar, Mali, Mauritius, Niger, Republic of Congo, Senegal, Seychelles.
Non-African countries: France, Canada, Luxembourg, Monaco, Switzerland, Vanuatu, Vietnam
Portuguese
African Countries: Angola, Cape Verde, Guinea-Bissau, Mozambique, Rwanda, Sao Tome and Principe.
Non-African countries: Portugal, Brazil, Cabo Verde, Timor-Leste
Swahili
African countries: Kenya, Mozambique, Tanzania, Uganda, Zambia

EDITORIAL
DESERTERS

The Christadelphian Tidings – Volume 87, Number 3 / March, 2024

HAVE you ever felt someone deserted you? Maybe it was a close friend you were depending on who wasn't there for you when needed. Perhaps you were working with someone on an important project, but they failed to execute their commitment. Or someone who didn't have the courage to stand with you when you were being tested.

Being a deserter is a pretty strong label. Being a deserter can bring harsh court martialing and punishment in military matters. In times of war, it could result in execution. Storybooks are filled with men and women who stand strong in courage, but they castigate those who run away in fear.

One man in Scripture was labeled a deserter–John Mark. His story is one we can take great comfort in. In it, we see rejection and separation, but eventually reconciliation and harmony. In Acts 15, when we read this, Paul and Barnabas were about to revisit the cities they had initially been preaching in.

> *Barnabas wanted to take John, also called Mark, with them, but Paul did not think it wise to take him, because **he had deserted them** in Pamphylia and had not continued with them in the work. They had such a sharp disagreement that they parted company. Barnabas took Mark and sailed for Cyprus.* (Acts 15:37-39 NIV).

Looking at this event historically, with 20/20 hindsight, the separation of Paul and Barnabas's daily partnership may have been necessary. In other words, this all worked for good. The benefit of Barnabas's wisdom and counsel for Paul may have been fully realized in God's plan. But this event certainly wasn't one of the best moments of the first century. Earlier, Barnabas had been *"carried away"* by those of the circumcision party in fear of eating with new Gentile believers (Gal 2:12-13). Yet, after Paul rebuked Peter for his hypocrisy (and, by implication, Barnabas), there was a willingness to examine their motives and reach accord. But in this case, they could find no agreement.

Barnabas was a man who believed in others. He was one of the first to believe in Paul after his conversion, staking his reputation that Paul's faith was genuine. Barnabas was the *"son of consolation,"* always looking for the best in others, counting that the Lord would lead good men and women to righteous acts.

Acts 13 briefly comments on the departure of John Mark. He had been taken with Paul and Barnabas from Jerusalem to Antioch, Seleucia, Cyprus (Barnabas's native land), Salamis, and the Isle of Paphos. When they were leaving Paphos, John departed and returned to Jerusalem.

But why did he leave? F. F. Bruce suggests one of the possible reasons involved the rigors of missionary work. But Bruce further suggests that it may have been possible that John Mark had resented how his cousin Barnabas had slipped to "second place" behind Paul. When the team set out to work, it was *"Barnabas and Saul."* (Acts 12:25). But when John Mark departed, the Bible referred to the team as *"Paul and his company."* (Acts 13:13).[1] Richard Rackham concluded that John Mark was far from a coward in his return to Jerusalem but was instead "unable to

tidings.org

5

keep pace with the rapid expansion of S. Paul's views of work in the Gentile world."[2] Further, one wonders if there was a personal reason for returning to Jerusalem, as we know that his mother, Mary, owned a house there. Did temporary family obligations bring him back home?

We don't have a specific reason for why John Mark left. Luke likely didn't know either, which is why he left the reason out of the Acts narrative. But Paul felt that the departure of John Mark was significant. It wasn't just a difference of opinion; more modern versions translate the disagreement as *"sharp."* There had been previous issues where Barnabas and Paul had had disagreements. But now, their difference in view about John Mark was so severe they determined to stop working together because of it.

However, in the end, John Mark didn't desert the gospel or neglect to serve the ecclesia. Only a few months later, he was again ready to rejoin the missionary work. When Paul and Barnabas split, John Mark journeyed with his cousin Barnabas to Cyprus to labor for the gospel there. We are left to wonder what role John Mark played while paired with his cousin and what counsel he may have received from the wise Levite.

While the Scriptural trail goes cold about Barnabas from this point forward, we do hear about John Mark.

In Colossians 4, we read:

Aristarchus, who is in prison with me, sends you his greetings, and so does Mark, Barnabas's cousin. As you were instructed before, make Mark welcome if he comes your way. (Col 4:10 NLT).

It appears John Mark was in Rome during Paul's first imprisonment, working with Paul once again. Paul instructed the Colossians to receive John Mark and welcome him. That's quite a transformation from the last time we saw these two men together. Whatever conflict had once existed between them appears to have been extinguished. These men embraced the Lord's teachings to work out their differences in love for the gospel's sake.

Writing to Timothy, in what is probably Paul's last epistle, he says,

Take Mark, and bring him with thee: for he is profitable to me for the ministry. (2 Tim 4:11).

He may also be the *"Marcus"* mentioned in Philemon as one of four *"fellowlabourers"* with Paul. The supposition is that the Gospel of Mark was written by John Mark, sourcing his information from the Apostle Peter in Jerusalem.

Lessons for Modern Times

There will inevitably be disagreements, broken commitments, and disappointments in ecclesial life. We

> In the end, John Mark didn't desert the gospel or neglect to serve the ecclesia. Only a few months later, he was again ready to rejoin the missionary work.

Editorial / Deserters

are but flesh, and we make mistakes. We mistakenly and unwisely judge motives and actions through an imperfect lens. When we predict future behavior based on what we have seen in the past, we fail to acknowledge the Lord is working in the other person's life. What is natural to the flesh is to walk away, divide, and label. "I won't work with them again!" "I can't trust them."

We should not assume intentions or motives with observed behavior. There are often hidden reasons for why we were let down. Sometimes, the reason may have been us! Maybe we were too hard to work with or too demanding. Often, we may later learn that the reasons for the misfire were completely unknown to us.

It would also have been extremely easy for John Mark to hold a deep grudge about Paul's rejection. It might have been understandable if he had chosen only to serve with his cousin and avoided dealings with Paul. To his credit, we find him in Rome when Paul is in greatest need.

I wonder what it was that brought Paul and John Mark back together. Who was it that encouraged them to unite in Rome? I suspect it may have been Barnabas. Barnabas, the apostle known for encouragement (Acts 4:36), possibly brokered the restoration. We need more brothers and sisters like Barnabas. Believers committed to breaking down barriers, encouraging conflict resolution, and mending the

Our own community's history teaches us that separation due to conflict solves nothing...

tidings.org

broken nets of ecclesial work. There is immense value in people like Barnabas who choose to see the best in others and encourage peace. As James wrote, *"Those who are peacemakers will plant seeds of peace and reap a harvest of righteousness."* (Jas 3:18 NLT).

Our own community's history teaches us that separation due to conflict solves nothing. It results in isolation and robs us of access to a critical part of the body. Conflict can sometimes pass down over generations and sour relations among believers. There are some we've avoided for decades. Groups that we have labeled as unreliable. People we feel we are better off without. It is hard, really hard, to attempt to reconcile when someone has hurt or condemned you. It seems much easier just to stop interacting or to interact in a way that superficially shows everything is okay when everyone knows it is not.

I suppose many of us need a trip with John Mark to Rome!

This concept was one of the Lord's first teachings.

> So if you are presenting a sacrifice at the altar in the Temple and you suddenly remember that someone has something against you, leave your sacrifice there at the altar. Go and be reconciled to that person. Then come and offer your sacrifice to God. "When you are on the way to court with your adversary, settle your differences quickly." (Matt 5:23-25 NLT).

Notice the urgency of Jesus' teaching. Do it right now! Reconciliation is more important than the offering you are about to make at the altar. In matters of conflict, time is almost always an enemy. Those we distrust will not become more trustable by avoidance. When we reconcile, it opens new doors for the work of our Lord, just as it did for Paul and John Mark.

The challenge of the gospel was never intended to be easy or to appeal to our natural impulses of the flesh. It is hard to subdue one's pride and seek restoration. It is unnatural to seek out someone who has hurt or disappointed you. But this is exactly what the Lord commands.

Because these men demonstrated the spirit of our Lord, Paul was able to rely on John Mark at a time when he was chained and imprisoned. The one who once left the ministry was now one of a handful essential to Paul's ongoing ministry. He was able to touch and serve those who Paul could not. We are also blessed with Mark's beautiful gospel that elegantly describes the compassion and service of our Lord.

How will your story change if you reconcile with those who have *"something against you?"* Are you willing to leave your comfortable religious observance (your gift at the altar) to go and attempt to reunite? If you are, we are all the beneficiaries.

Dave Jennings

---

[1] Bruce, F. F., *Commentary on the Book of Acts*, Wm. B. Eerdmans Publishing Company, Grand Rapids, MI, 1956.
[2] Rackham, Richard Belward, *The Acts of the Apostles*, Methuen & Company, London, 1904.

LIFE APPLICATION

DEBORAH AND JAEL
LEADING BY EXAMPLE AS SERVANTS

By Sophie Robinson

At a sister's class recently, I was discussing with friends how lessons from faithful individuals still apply today in what can sometimes seem like a vastly different world. While God may not require us to take some of the physical actions of those in the biblical record, such as driving a tent peg through a man's skull or calling thousands of men to war, we are certainly able to study and apply the principles behind these actions. Judges chapter 4 is a record of two women who illustrate the Christlike character and willing attitude we can take on when serving God in our own lives. Jael and Deborah's accounts show it is God who works through us and the miraculous outcomes that can be when we allow him to do just that.

In Judges, as the name suggests, we see God bringing up judges to lead the people of Israel. Through their cycles of sin, struggle, repentance, and being lifted out of captivity by God, these judges act as a conduit to God for the children of Israel. At this time, God had set up the Judge and Prophetess, Deborah in this position of influence and power within the nation. (See Judges 4:4-5 and the "Psalm of Deborah" in Judges 5).

> Now Deborah, a prophetess, the wife of Lapidoth, was judging Israel at that time. She used to sit under the palm of Deborah between Ramah and Bethel in the hill country of Ephraim, and the people of Israel came up to her for judgment." (Judg 4:4-5 ESV).[1]

Deborah as *"the wife of Lapidoth,"* has taken on this name that means "burning torch or firebrand." Considering this, perhaps the verse implies that Deborah is a firebrand of a woman judging Israel at that time, as it becomes a perfect description of the role she plays for the people of Israel.

This year, in our ecclesia's youth group, one of our study topics was practical service. It is clear this work can come in various forms, such as spiritual motivation, physical acts of service, and emotional support for our brothers and sisters. In Judges 4:9, we read that Deborah states that Barak would win the battle, but the fate of the Canaanite commander would be put into the hands of a woman. Barak assumes this woman is Deborah when, in fact, it is Jael. One might derive negative connotations about Barak from this exchange, but we should note that Barak agrees wholeheartedly to go alongside Deborah and Hebrews 11:32 later lists him as one of the faithful. This teamwork and reliance on a godly woman by a faithful man is a great example to us as we seek to support each other in the ecclesia, in relations, or even in the CYC. We have the same ability to encourage our brothers and sisters by placing God and Scripture at the forefront of our speech, decisions, and actions.

Barak and Deborah head off into battle, leading five of the tribes of Israel against Sisera and his great army. At this point, we clearly see God assisting Deborah and Barak. We are reminded He is always with us also to help fight our daily "battles":

> The LORD discomfited Sisera and all his chariots, and all his host, with the edge of the sword before Barak; so that Sisera lighted down off his chariot, and fled away on his feet… and all the host of Sisera fell upon the edge of the sword, and there was not a man left. (Judg 4:15).

Sisera, once a mighty leader of the host who had persecuted and oppressed the people of God for twenty years, flees as the Israelites destroy his army. Weary, he comes to the tent of Heber and Jael, the Kenites. If we investigate the ancestry of Heber and, by extension, Jael, it illuminates the character and mindset of this inspirational family. Heber was a descendant of Jethro, who was a priest of Midian. His other name was "Reuel" (Exod 2:18), which means "a friend of God." In Numbers 10, we see Jethro's appointed role for Israel:

> And he said unto him, I will not go; but I will depart to mine own land, and to my kindred. And he said, Leave us not, I pray thee; forasmuch as thou knowest how we are to encamp in the wilderness, **and thou mayest be to us instead of eyes.** And it shall be, if thou go with us, yea, it shall be, that what goodness the LORD shall do unto us, the same will we do unto thee. (Num 10:30-32).

Life Application / Deborah and Jael: Leading by Example as Servants

Jael marries Heber and becomes part of this family whose appointed role was to be eyes for the Israelites in the wilderness. This alliance is a splendid example for us in our ecclesias and community—we all greatly benefit from looking out for each other as we journey and wrestle with "wilderness experiences" en route to God's Kingdom. It also provides some helpful context as we study the account more deeply.

When Sisera comes to the tent of Jael, he begs for provisions but then is stopped dead in his tracks:

> *Then Jael Heber's wife took a nail of the tent, and took a hammer in her hand, and went softly unto him, and smote the nail into his temples, and fastened it into the ground: for he was fast asleep and weary. So he died. And, behold, as Barak pursued Sisera, Jael came out to meet him.* (Judg 4:21-22).

These two verses appear to describe everything that happened in that tent. Jael feeds Sisera; she puts him to sleep; she fastens his head to the ground with a tent peg. And then Barak arrives on the scene. In Judges 5, Deborah commends Jael for this brave act:

> *Blessed above women shall Jael the wife of Heber the Kenite be, blessed shall she be above women in the tent... She put her hand to the nail, and her right hand to the workmen's hammer; and with the hammer she smote Sisera, she smote off his head, when she had pierced and stricken through his temples. At her feet he bowed, he fell, he lay down: at her feet he bowed, he fell: where he bowed, there he fell down dead.* (Judg 5:24-27).

However, when we compare Judges 4:21 with Deborah's retelling of the event in Judges 5:24-27, it becomes apparent that there are several significant differences regarding what happened in Jael's tent. In Judges 4, the text is quite specific: Sisera was *"fast asleep"* when she hit the tent peg so deeply into his temple that she fastened him to the ground. So why does Deborah's account paint a different picture in the next chapter? She tells of Sisera, this

tidings.org

captain of sin, bowing and falling down dead at Jael's feet. The explanation is likely that Deborah, a woman very well-versed in God's word, is trying to bring our minds to a powerful lesson that echoes throughout scripture.

Deborah uses the phrase *"fell down and bowed"* three times in quick succession. This phrase appears forty-four times in scripture to show obeisance, in thankfulness, in death and in praise. In all these instances, the phrase *"fell down"* has some relation to God's power and His hand at work. For example:

> *They shall bow down to thee with their face toward the earth, and lick up the dust of thy feet and thou shalt know that I am the LORD.* (Isa 49:23).

Another well-known Bible story employs this same expression:

> *And all this assembly shall know that the LORD saveth not with sword and spear: for the battle is the LORD'S, and he will give you into our hands... And David put his hand in his bag, and took thence a stone, and slang it, and smote the Philistine in his forehead, that the stone sunk into his forehead; and he fell upon his face to the earth.* (1 Sam 17:47, 49).

Note the similarities: the stone had sunk into Goliath's forehead just as the tent peg went through Sisera's temple, and Goliath fell upon his face to the earth just as Sisera was fastened to the ground by the nail. Deborah elaborates that Jael had *"smitten off his head,"* which is not included in the first account of Sisera's death, just as David had used Goliath's sword to take off the head of this giant who had defied the armies of the living God. Furthermore, David became angry at the people for not standing up to a man who defied God (1 Sam 17:26), in much the same way that Jael stood up to Sisera in a time when many others *"had not come to the help of the LORD."* (Judg 5:23).

Some other examples include the unclean spirits that fell down before Jesus (Mark 3:11) and the idol Dagon, that was fallen and *"the head of Dagon and both the palms of its hands were broken off on the threshold; only Dagon's torso was left of it."* (1 Sam 5:4). Once again, we see an idol of the nations brought low to the earth before God's will. In these examples, sin is brought low in an instant, falling down to the earth in front of these types of Christ to show that the war was of God. This concept is also a good reminder for us to bow ourselves sincerely and faithfully before the God of Israel rather than becoming part of the Image of Men seen in Daniel's vision, which will eventually topple to the ground and be crushed into powder by Christ (Dan 2:35).

I would like to proceed to look at both Deborah and Jael, the faithful women who conquered God's enemies for Israel, to see how the lessons from their lives apply to each of us. The Book of Judges depicts Deborah as a Judge, a prophetess, and a leader. Deborah also chose to describe herself as a *"mother in Israel"* (Judg 5:7), which inspires us to understand that a mother can also be a Judge, a warrior, and a nurturing leader. This comforting leadership is also shown by God (Isa 49:15; 66:13).

Life Application / Deborah and Jael: Leading by Example as Servants

Deborah did not seek leadership in battle; however, Barak and his army would not go up to the battle without this Godly woman at their head.

I will meet them as a bear that is bereaved of her whelps, and will rend the caul of their heart, and there will I devour them like a lion: the wild beast shall tear them. (Hos 13:8).

Christ also models this mother-like characteristic. We read in Matthew 23:37 that he would have gathered the children of Israel together as a hen gathers her chickens under her wings if the people had been willing.

For Deborah, arising as a mother in Israel meant taking action and initiative, reminding the people of God's word, conveying God's message to Barak (Judges 4:6) and, when it was needed, helping to lead the people herself. She did not seek leadership in battle; however, Barak and his army would not go up to the battle without this godly woman at their head. This Christlike attitude of being ready and willing to lead by example is one that we should incorporate into our own lives and in our ecclesias. Deborah also provided a source of motivation and firm "nudging" to Barak to take on the leadership role that God desired from him. Do we practice these same mother-like qualities in our ecclesias and encourage and motivate each other to take leadership roles?

In Numbers 10:29-32, we read earlier that Moses asked Jethro to become *"eyes to the Israelites"* in the wilderness. In Scripture, eyes often symbolize light entering the body. For example, the eyes of Eli, the priest, became cloudy as his faith and service to God weakened. As an additional example, the Apostle Paul lost and regained his sight as he was shown the truth and turned to God. Jesus uses this same imagery to develop exhortations for our lives:

The light of the body is the eye: if therefore thine eye be single, thy whole body shall be full of light; but if thine eye be evil, thy whole body shall be full of darkness. (Matt 6:22-23, Luke 11:34 KJV).

We see in Jael a working out of the legacy of the Kenites. Her brave act not only mirrored the work of her ancestor, Jethro but was also a light to the whole body of Israel and a sign of God's power over sin for all to see:

And then, as Barak pursued Sisera, Jael came out to meet him, and said to him, "Come, I will show you the man whom you seek." And when he went into her tent, there lay Sisera, dead with the peg in his temple. So on that day God subdued Jabin king of Canaan in the presence of the children of Israel. (Judg 4:22-23).

tidings.org

Jael saw and took the opportunity to serve God and stand on His side. In Judges 4, we find a curious note about King Jabin, whose forces Sisera commanded:

> Sisera fled away on his feet to the tent of Jael the wife of Heber the Kenite: for there was peace between Jabin the king of Hazor and the house of Heber the Kenite. (Judg 4:17).

Strangely, we learn that Jael's house (or perhaps her husband?) was at peace with this oppressor of the Israelites. But Jael was given the choice to put her trust in God or side with and obtain the favor of these ruling powers. When the opportunity arose to strike Sisera down, she immediately acted. She knew in whose hand the battle belonged and who Sisera, the captain of the hosts, would be falling down before. Given the same choices in our personal lives, do we act with the same decisiveness and allegiance to God and His people?

We can trace Jael's confidence back to the assurance of her husband's grandfather, Jethro, who was the father-in-law to Moses:

> And Moses told his father-in-law all that the LORD had done unto Pharaoh and to the Egyptians for Israel's sake, and all the travail that had come upon them by the

We are called to be a light or a "burning torch" to our brothers and sisters, to recognize where we have the chance to serve God, to be an uplifting and passionate example to those around us...

The Christadelphian Tidings – Volume 87, Number 3 / March, 2024

Life Application / Deborah and Jael: Leading by Example as Servants

way, and how the LORD delivered them... And Jethro said, Blessed be the LORD... **Now I know that the LORD is greater than all gods; for in the thing wherein they dealt proudly he was above them.** (Exod 18:8-12).

Jethro, a Gentile convert to the God of Israel, believed that God works for and through us in our lives. God alone can conquer sin, and when we choose to stand for Him, He will work through us to show this, making us a light to the world.

So in Christ Jesus you are all children of God through faith, for all of you who were baptized into Christ have clothed yourselves with Christ. There is neither Jew nor Gentile, neither slave nor free, nor is there male and female, for you are all one in Christ Jesus. If you belong to Christ, then you are Abraham's seed, and heirs according to the promise. (Gal 3:26-29 NIV).

Each of us has been called to act in the image of God. We are called to be a light or a "burning torch" to our brothers and sisters, to recognize where we have the chance to serve God, to be an uplifting and passionate example to those around us, and to be faithful individuals that God can work with and use to show His glory.

But ye are a chosen generation, a royal priesthood, an holy nation a peculiar people: that ye should show forth the praises of him who hath called you out of the darkness into his marvelous light which in times past were not a people but now are a people of God: which had not obtained mercy but have now obtained mercy. (1 Pet 2:9-10).

By following the example of those who obeyed and pleased God, we can become heirs according to these same promises. Jael knew the power of God, and it inspired her to make faithful decisions that had a major impact on the whole nation of Israel. Deborah, having God's word written in her heart and mind, acted as a mother of Israel to help lead them to victory over the nations who had persecuted God's people.

Likewise, God provides us opportunities to shine and stand for him and is always there to help us fight our battles. He is at our sides continually and has promised that we can bring sin low into submission, so we must keep His Scripture ready in our hearts and minds. When we take action prayerfully, guided by God's Word, to have a positive spiritual impact, God will provide the victory.

Sophie Robinson,
Cambridge Ecclesia, ON

---

1 All Scriptural citations are taken from the New King James Version, unless specifically noted.

SPECIAL SECTION: PERSONAL PREACHING

170 YEARS OF PREACHING IN NORTH AMERICA

By Peter Hemingray

THIS article covers the attempts and various methods used by organizations, ecclesias and individuals to preach to the public. These methods invariably require individual members to bring those interested to truly know the gospel message. But this duty, although a vital part of each individual's responsibility, is outside the scope of what I will cover. Also, many ecclesias have done immense work themselves to spread the gospel, but these valuable endeavors are far too numerous to cover in a brief article. So, I must, by and large, cover efforts that took place among multiple ecclesias.

Early Years

In 1854, 170 years ago, John Thomas visited near Henderson, Kentucky, located near the southwestern corner of Indiana. It was at the invitation of J. T. Norment, who had read *Elpis Israel*. This request prompted Dr. Thomas to make an eight-day journey, mostly by riverboat along the Ohio River, without any opportunity to change clothes. John Thomas gave a series of lectures there. And so, a typical early little ecclesia slowly formed, which still exists deep in rural Indiana.

As these little ecclesias developed, they found it essential to hire halls (or sometimes build them) to proclaim the gospel, which they usually did by advertising evening lectures in the local newspapers. Many of the existing advertisements of the time that can be found simply publicized Dr. John Thomas as a lecturer. Detroit in 1866 is the earliest "Christadelphian" ecclesia I can find that simply advertised their evening lectures.[1] And so the tradition of evening lectures intending to invite "interested friends" to listen to Bible Topics was underway in North America.

The ecclesias often held evening lectures. Others that did not, customarily held special efforts periodically, particularly when visiting speakers arrived. When Robert Roberts came through in 1871, he attracted large audiences of over 400, but only when they heavily advertised his lectures. As he said,

> America may differ from England. An advertisement in a paper is not sufficient to attract attention to a lecture in England. We always issue large posters and handbills, in addition to advertisements, and in this way secure large audiences. We are persuaded America would be no exception as regards this result. At all points of the American tour, wherever effective publicity was given to the meetings, there were large audiences; and at all places where the announcement, or place of meeting was inadequate, the attendance was poor.[2]

An example of individual proclamation of the message was that of R. T. S.

Powell of Hamilton, Ontario.

> He [was] indefatigable in his efforts to call his neighbors' attention to the truth, which his connection with the town, from youth upwards, has favored. He has canvassed his townsmen right and left, to subscribe to the Christadelphian. The result is a list of about 50 subscribers in Hamilton alone.[3]

Christian literature has been the main approach to preaching the message and establishing contacts for about a century. When ecclesias were more established, personal contact and well-advertised public lectures were used. In fact, I can remember delivering a lecture in the mid-1990s in a local library, not the ecclesial hall, on how archeology confirms the Bible. About a dozen visitors stayed to talk, so the method was still working at that time. Unfortunately, advertising via the newspaper is no longer effective, and almost no one responds to hand-delivered or mailed flyers. As far as I can tell, only a few North American ecclesias hold a Sunday evening lecture, although two or three have Bible Hours or similar on Sunday afternoons. Even in the UK, evening lectures have almost disappeared during this century. But it is a little sad that evening lectures have gone, as they served a useful purpose for our unbaptized children who mostly only heard the "first principles" taught in a systematic way by listening to them expounded during these lectures.

The Bible Truth

On rare occasions, you might come across old dusty *Christadelphian* magazines, and even more rarely, one called *"Bible Truth."* It was the work of one brother, Gustav Aue, a prosperous coal merchant from New Jersey, and was almost totally a preaching magazine, like the *Glad Tidings* of the UK today. It seems to have been published primarily by himself. He issued it from 1911 to 1935, and I would estimate he distributed nearly one million copies. Few remain, and as Bro. Gustav was opposed to Bro. Strickler's teachings, he limited its circulation after 1923 solely to the "Berean" ecclesias in North America. There are reports of a few baptisms directly associated with its circulation, but one hopes the million distributed had a significant impact.

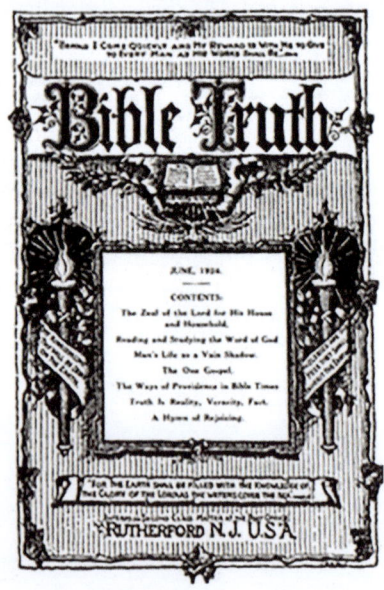

New Initiatives Start[4]

Unlike in the UK, there were locally coordinated preaching efforts in North America in the 1960s. Although many new approaches were tried from the 1930s on, it is difficult to identify their success. However, we will look at a few areas where individuals or many brethren and sisters were involved. The period of the 1950s is difficult to cover succinctly, for many individuals were involved somewhat independently, and many organizations to help with preaching, both locally and continent-wide, came into existence at least for a while. In addition, the CBM in the UK was involved, at least from 1956 to 1968.

Vacation Bible Campaigns

In the UK, a grassroots movement by university students commenced. They held a concentrated preaching effort in 1935, with eight members holding lectures, accompanied by advertising posters, canvassing door-to-door and bill distribution, open-air speakers, and sandwich board processions. This movement spread rapidly, and the campaign movement continues in the UK today. So, when John Carter, Editor of *The Christadelphian Magazine*, came to North America in 1953, he encouraged a group to organize teams of workers to go door-to-door with thousands of leaflets. Some campaigners went to work in the Baltimore area on the three-day Memorial Day weekend of 1954. They began with a campaign in Canton, Ohio, with Bro. A. D. Norris. Other ecclesias and campaign committees started, including one in Victoria, BC, but no national committee existed. In the years 1954-1960, additional door-to-door campaigns were held in Moorestown, NJ, Meriden, CT, Canton, OH, and again in Baltimore. Other campaign committees and ecclesias held events, particularly on the West Coast, Texas, and British Columbia. The ALS and Christadelphian Bible Society (CBS) assisted some of these campaigns.

Later, in 1970, the Southern California ecclesias, under the aegis of the Pacific Coast Christadelphian Bible Mission, initiated a program called Truth Corps. Its first goal was to help with preaching in Panama City, Panama, where, for nine weeks, eight members canvassed and set up Bible Classes in homes. This concept expanded to Lompoc, CA, in 1973, where eleven members spent five weeks. At the end of this effort, sixteen people were studying for baptism.

Truth Corps helped more than in the immediate preaching support; it increased the focus of the ecclesia on preaching and reaching out to their local communities. However, the main benefit of Truth Corps was in the spiritual growth of the team members. After observing a Truth Corps team member upon his return, a brother mentioned that it effected five years of spiritual growth in him during that summer. When someone returned from their Truth Corps experience, they were different. They had spent a summer living in close contact with others, sharing in the household duties, putting up with the inconveniences in a crowded house, and spending a good part of each day generating and visiting contacts with a presentation and other preaching activities. Added to this was the close and intimate discussion of their experiences as a team. Spiritual growth was almost inevitable.

ALS and ASK Movement

The North American Branch of the UK ALS (Auxiliary Lecturing Society) began in 1955, with eight Ontario and two US border ecclesias. Various efforts were held in Canada for the next few years, with some campaigns organized. The only active branch appears to have been in the Pacific Northwest, but there seems to be no activity after 1970.

In April 1961, *The Christadelphian Magazine* carried this news item:

> Perhaps the most significant news out of New England for 1960 and for many previous years, is the formation of a joint committee by the ecclesias here, named A.S.K. for the Advancement of Scripture Knowledge. The purpose of this committee is to expand the work of the ecclesias here into all of New England... We hope that others will be encouraged by the formation of this group to press their efforts into the great voids of the U.S.A.[5]

The ASK (Advancement of Scriptural Knowledge) name was quickly embraced by the brotherhood. It came to be associated with a wide range of preaching initiatives, and additional "ASK Committees" appeared in several parts of North America. While the ASK movement has not filled much of the ecclesial voids of New England or anywhere else in the past 50 years, it has produced some lasting results and has fired much enthusiasm for preaching. The latter has been one of its strong points. One brother put his finger on a vital reason for ASK's success. He identified the emphasis on personal preaching, cooperation between workers in all stages of the scheme, and the contagious enthusiasm of each individual.

The New England ASK and the Mid-Atlantic ASK were both active for many years. New England sponsored a trailer and a booth at the Eastern States Exposition from 1970 until 1990. Both organizations appear to have been affected by the COVID-19 pandemic.

Across the border in Canada, the Great Lakes ASK was formed in 1969 and still is active in the Toronto area. In the Maritimes, the Atlantic Provinces section was formed in 2006 and is still active among the remote, scattered ecclesias in that area.

Work by the UK CBM and the Christadelphian Bible Society (CBS)

Soon after the formation of the UK Christadelphian Bible Mission (CBM) in 1955, its attention turned to the North American continent, where so many states and provinces had so few, if any, Christadelphians. In 1956,

Dennis Ford (1928-1961)

Bro. A. D. Norris attended a campaign along the English style in Canton, Ohio, with a dozen campaigners. In addition, a little later, newspaper advertising in areas remote from any ecclesia was started, offering correspondence courses in association with the work of Bro. Dennis Ford of the Pittsburgh Ecclesia. In 1961, Bro. Ford started the Christadelphian Bible Society, CBS, which published a newsletter detailing the efforts supported by the CBM in the USA. The major effort was the work in Piketon, OH, a town in the middle of Ohio, more than 200 miles from any ecclesia. Many visitors attended the lectures held in a rented building, but by 1965, interest dwindled. Despite the sad death of Bro. and Sis. Ford in a car accident in 1961 on the way to Piketon, the work of CBS continued in newspaper advertising, with some success. One individual could accomplish so much. Still, the need for collaboration of effort is evident as they saw the work on the East Coast slow down.

In 1968, *The Bible Missionary* reported:

> Cooperation with other Christadelphian preaching organizations in North America is planned, and a joint committee with the North American Auxiliary Lecturing Society, and the New England Advancement of Scripture Knowledge (A.S.K.) group, has been formed. A joint fund for co-operative projects is being considered, and if this leads to positive results, it may be possible to relieve the Bible Mission of its share of responsibility for the work of the Bible Society.[6]

Most of the involvement of the UK CBM with the work in North America ended. Still, happily, the CBMA (Christadelphian Bible Mission America) and CBMC (Christadelphian Bible Mission Canada) were soon formed.

Bible Seminars

One would be hard-pressed to find a single development in the past 25 years that has had more impact on ecclesial outreach than the Bible seminar programs. Initiated in 1992 in the North Industry Ecclesia (now Paris Avenue) in Ohio, the seminars have largely changed the frame of reference for many ecclesias about outreach possibilities in their communities.

During the next few years, with no real organization or formal structure, the concept of Bible seminars swept rapidly across North America and elsewhere. Ecclesias, which found public lectures poorly attended despite persistent and

faithful efforts instead, encountered an enthusiastic reception by the public of the *"Learn to Read the Bible Effectively"* seminar.

Over time, the seminar concept has been modified, and new courses have emerged to meet students' interests. Many ecclesias made the seminar an annual part of their preaching program, supplemented with other important outreach activities. Ecclesias benefitted from the fruit of the seminars, including new members and an exciting new focus on the first principle truths that we hold dear.

Seminars work best with extensive advertising, which indicates the seminar is free for anyone who wants to "Learn To Read The Bible Effectively" and covers twelve weeks at the same time and place each week. Advertising also usually includes a map, a phone number to register with a real live person, and a mail-in form if they prefer not to call. Locations can be either a public hall or the local ecclesial hall. Although using a public hall can attract more attendees, it is less likely the initial attendees will attend follow-up sessions when held in the ecclesial hall.

Much written material is available, both for the beginning seminar and follow-up seminars, and these seminars are also available as videos. PowerPoint slides, student handbooks, and a teacher's manual give suggested scripts. Most information available online at present is designed for a student, not for an ecclesia starting a seminar, but most websites will supply material if contacted.

Bible Exhibitions

In the UK, a Bible exhibition has been a regular yearly feature of many campaigns since about 1964. But in North America, it was 1985 before the Victoria, BC Ecclesia erected a similar one. More recently, Bro. Paul Billington in Ontario developed an exhibit, which is still occasionally used in Canada and neighboring US states. Although it is costly and requires much ecclesial effort, it has always been quite a successful draw, especially when linked with the 400th anniversary of the KJV Bible.

Radio and TV Work

Preaching via the radio began early in the United States and Canada. By 1927, a radio station in Seattle broadcast lectures every Sunday; this outreach continued for decades. At one stage, ten radio stations across the continent carried regular broadcasts at various times and days. In the 1970s, such methods transitioned into a half-hour TV program on Sunday afternoons, which, in Southern California, meant the programs were expensive to produce. For decades, renting a studio and hiring a director and professional staff was necessary to get a finished product.

With the advent of cable networks in the 1980s, the Southern California Radio-TV Committee found a new and lower-cost way to carry on with television broadcasting by taking advantage of public access channels and producing their own programs. After renting a TV studio for a day and building a set, a professional director led the five speakers through their sessions. The public access stations enabled the committee to use free airtime, but even so, the production costs were considerable for the studio equipment and hired staff.

Partnering with Bro. Jeff Wallace of the Boston Ecclesia in the 1990s, the next approach was to put together taping sessions to produce 26 programs each over a long weekend. The process in Boston was repeated in Houston, Pittsburgh, Detroit, Toronto, and Los Angeles. By purchasing advanced editing equipment, programs could now be assembled and edited at home instead of hiring an expensive studio.

This work continued for several years, but with the widespread use of low-cost video technology and the Internet, the use of studio videos seems to have almost disappeared by about 2007. How effective the recent proliferation of available Christadelphian videos is in preaching is unknown, but modern technology has a role to play in our preaching. Exactly how to implement it is up to the newer generations.

Social Media

Many North American ecclesias have web pages, and some of these have preaching information. There are also many ecclesial Facebook pages. Some of our brothers and sisters are just beginning to discover how Artificial Intelligence (AI) may be able to improve our preaching work.

Summary

If history teaches us anything, it is that change is ever with us. The only certain foundation is the Bible and its message. The message does not change, but how we spread it has and will continue to change. As some avenues close (evening lectures, newspaper advertising), others have opened and will continue to open. How we use them is reliant on ecclesial and individual efforts, with almost no regional or national support.

Peter Hemingray,
Pittsburgh Ecclesia, PA

---

1 John Thomas wrote his Constitution in 1854, including an order of service, but does not mention public lectures.
2 *The Christadelphian*, 1871 p. 349.
3 Op. cit, p. 248. See same quotation in Hamilton Greenaway Ecclesia Centennial article in this issue.
4 A *Tidings* Special Issue on "Preaching in North America," August 2011, provided much of the information here.
5 *The Christadelphian*, 1961, p. 181.
6 *The Bible Missionary*, June 1968, p. 31.

SPECIAL SECTION: PERSONAL PREACHING

ONE BROTHER'S STORY

By Larry Sherfield

THERE are moments in our lives that stand out as pivotal, shaping the course of our existence. Walking across the stage, diploma in hand. Saying "I do" at the altar. Becoming a parent. These moments aren't a flash of time but rather a culmination of many moments in gradual succession. Of course, some moments result in triumphs and some in setbacks. Coming to know the Truth was no different for me. I took a gradual path from introduction to the Bible until I was fully immersed in water, surrounded by a crowd of brothers and sisters who all understood my joy. At that time, some of them may have even reflected on their own baptisms. On the day of my baptism, I was 40 years old.

I did not get there entirely on my own, however. By God's grace, I was fortunate enough to meet someone at age 17 who became my friend and was willing to personally witness to me whether it seemed like a cool thing to do or not. I believe that personal witnesses can come in many forms. I have heard anecdotes expressing how God works in one's life—diving into Scripture with someone to find answers and encountering people who lead by example. These influences were effective and had their place in my journey to the Truth.

Rewind about 22 years before the day of my baptism to find a typical teenager and senior in high school. High school is a time of exploration and self-discovery; for me, it became the starting point of a spiritual journey. A friend shared with me Bible teachings common in the Christadelphian community, which piqued my interest. Curiosity naturally led me to ask questions. My friend's father, a knowledgeable figure deeply rooted in Scripture, patiently and warmly answered some of these questions. My friend and his father provided two categories of answers over several years. The first type was in the form of personal accounts of how God has worked in their lives. The other type of answer was straight from Scripture. This interaction was a model for searching the Bible for answers to life questions.

A couple of years later, I went with my friend to a Tuesday night course on understanding how to read the Bible offered by the ecclesia he and his family attended. As I met some members and collected my course materials, I could not help but notice feeling a bit nervous. As the night began, the speaker said a prayer and then stated that the intention of the 4-week course was not necessarily to preach doctrine; rather, the intent was to provide an understanding of what the Bible was and how to study it.

There were members of the ecclesia who made themselves available to answer questions. I was very pleased with what all of them said in one part of our conversations or another. Their different approach was something that I had not heard from any of the churches I went to with my family in the past. They emphasized that we should read the Bible ourselves and not take anyone's word on what to believe. They assisted me in looking up verses, not answering my questions with their words but rather with the Word of God.

Life has a way of testing our resolve, and for me, a particularly challenging period became the catalyst for a renewed spiritual exploration. The loss of both my uncle and grandmother within the same week to brain cancer shook the foundations of my emotional well-being. Simultaneously, the demanding nature of my role as a prison officer added a layer of stress, leaving me grappling with anxiety. As a new husband and father, the weight of responsibilities seemed insurmountable.

I found myself turning to prayer. I began by clutching a small KJV Bible that was a gift from my grandmother years before while I prayed to God in hopes of being heard. Pretty soon, I was opening the Bible in search of the comfort I somehow knew could only come from God. My first search? I searched out how I should pray. As I read Christ's words repeatedly, I unintentionally memorized the Lord's prayer.

Looking to increase my understanding of the Bible and refine my approach to prayer, I stumbled upon the Christadelphian "This is your Bible" online platform. It offered a structured program that promised a guide to understanding Scripture and a supportive community of believers. Enrolling in the program marked a turning point in my spiritual journey. Correspondence with a dedicated Bible teacher clarified intricate passages and guided me in building a good foundation for further Bible study. While I corresponded with this Bible teacher, I felt supported and encouraged in my search for the Truth. I was also encouraged to attend the closest ecclesia. However, my work schedules at the time and for years before never offered the opportunity to attend regularly. I worked shifts and weekends for many years. This circumstance was a setback in my mind.

Years later, I moved back to the California Central Coast from out of state, where I moved with my family for employment and educational opportunities. I could finally have a regular work week. That meant I could attend meeting on Sundays and classes mid-week evenings. Rediscovering the San Luis Obispo ecclesia became a homecoming, where I found a physical community and a spiritual family that embraced me with open arms.

These ecclesial members personally witnessed to me by the example of their lives. While Christ is the prime example we should strive to follow, initially, we who are new to the Truth do not fully understand how to be Christlike. Members of the ecclesia exemplified how a follower of Christ should live and treat others. The ecclesia proved to be a welcoming and inviting community. Their emphasis on personal Bible study struck a chord with me, reinforcing that understanding comes through a genuine search for truth. No one seemed to impose their beliefs on me or my family; instead, the ethos was rooted in supporting individual journeys and offering guidance.

Gratitude fills my heart for the transformative power of Scripture, prayer, and the supportive community that embraced me during challenging times. Reflecting on this journey, I am compelled to encourage others to explore their spiritual paths, seek solace in the teachings that resonate with their hearts, and find comfort in communities that foster genuine connections. My journey to truth is an ongoing narrative, a testament to the profound impact that faith, fellowship, and a true understanding of the gospel message can have on one's life. It has been and continues to be lived in many moments, leading to the life-saving grace only found with God in our dear Lord, Jesus.

Larry Sherfield,
San Luis Obispo Ecclesia, CA

EXHORTATION AND CONSOLATION

THE WHITE SPACE

By Jim Sullivan

I had a problem. Maybe some of you can relate to it. It was my turn to exhort, and I had no idea what I would talk about. I had taken all the usual steps. I looked at the readings for the day, but nothing was grabbing me. I perused prior exhortations I'd given in the hope of inspiration, but there was none. I prayed a little. I panicked a lot. I hoped I'd come down with the flu, but all to no avail. Then, amid total exasperation, I stumbled upon a couple of videos online from a certain Jewish rabbi, and from these, I found inspiration.

The rabbi was a fairly young man, maybe in his thirties, and he had produced (and continues to produce) a series of 10–15-minute videos about his Jewish faith. The first video was about the Jewish perspective on Christianity.

tidings.org 27

Speaking to his fellow Jews, he said this (I'm paraphrasing, but you'll get the idea):

As Jews, we have little to nothing to do with Christianity. We don't teach it in our schools, we don't talk about it in our synagogues, we don't really give it much thought at all. The reason for this is very easy to understand. We believe that the fundamental principle of Christianity is at odds with the fundamental principle of Judaism. The fundamental principle of Judaism is that the LORD God is one, whereas the fundamental principle of Christianity is that God is three. Christianity tries to say that three is actually one and one is three (which they refer to as 'trinity'), but the fact is you don't get to play around with the numbers. God is one. The Messiah is not God, the spirit of God is not God, only God is God, and everything else we believe emanates from this principle. So, we have always passed off Christianity as blasphemy because if your foundational principle is wrong, then everything else built upon it is going to be wrong as well. So, we leave Christianity over there, and we stay over here and as far as we're concerned, never the twain shall meet. But I learned something recently that blew me away and forces us, Jews, to look at certain Christians differently than we ever looked at any Christians before. I recently discovered there are people who consider themselves Christians who do not believe in the "Trinity." They believe that Jesus of Nazareth, who came and died over 2000 years ago, is the Messiah. They're wrong, of course [his words, not mine], but they do believe he was a man and not God. Now, I want you to consider what this means. Over the centuries, many Jews have believed

that one certain individual or another was the promised Messiah. Ultimately, they have always been proved wrong, but we did not cast them out as blasphemers. We still considered them Jews, just misinformed Jews. Therefore, we must consider these "Christians" not as blasphemers but simply as misguided fellow Jews.

The reason why this rabbi says that Jesus of Nazareth is not the proclaimed Messiah is because Jews believe that when the Messiah comes, he will immediately initiate the Kingdom age on earth. The rabbi claimed that nowhere in the Hebrew Bible does it teach that the Messiah would first die and then return and establish the Kingdom. We, of course, know there are several references to the death and return of the Messiah in the Hebrew Bible. For instance, a simple look at the timeline of Isaiah 53 clearly shows that the Messiah must die and then return, but that idea touches upon the subject of his second presentation that I was blessed to watch.

In his second video, he starts by holding up an open Hebrew Bible and says (paraphrased again, of course):

> This is a holy book, given to us by the very hand of the Almighty. Every space in this book is sacred. Now, on each page, words in black ink are written on a white background. We can read these words, comprehend what they say and gain understanding from them, but all around these words, between the lines and the letters, even underneath the black ink, there is "white space." Right now, we cannot comprehend what is revealed in this white space. That means there are major revelations in this holy book that have yet to be revealed. We believe, as devout Jews, that when the Messiah comes, he will reveal to us the glorious messages found in this white space.

Now, he wasn't suggesting for a minute that this "white space" has been revealed to anyone else. But we are blessed to know that it has because we know that the true Messiah has come and, by the grace of God, has revealed to his disciples the many beautiful revelations found in the white space. This glorious message is in, around, and underneath the words written on God's holy pages. The "white space" is nothing more than the spiritual truths written in black ink on the pages of the Word of Truth.

There are innumerable examples of the white space found throughout Scripture, whether from the words of Jesus or the interpretations of Paul and others. Even the lessons we hear every Sunday from those speakers who are blessed to see the white space! Here are just a few we can consider showing that the very "revelations" the rabbi desires have already been revealed by the Messiah, who came to those who believe in him in spirit and truth.

In Matthew 22, Jesus asks the Pharisees:

> *What think ye of Christ? Whose son is he? They say unto him, The Son of David. He saith unto them,*

The one who recognizes that the Word of God is holy and true places God's word above their own opinion and prejudices.

How then doth David in spirit call him Lord, saying, The LORD said unto my Lord, Sit thou on my right hand, till I make thine enemies thy footstool?' If David then calls him Lord, how is he his son? And no man was able to answer him a word, neither durst any man from that day forth ask him any more questions. (Matt 22:42-46).

The fact that they refused to ask any more questions proves two things. First, they understood that David, as the Messiah's "father," would not naturally refer to his later kin as his LORD, as the former is always blessed by the latter, not vice versa. But it also proves that they had no idea of the right answer. They couldn't comprehend the "white space" hidden from them because they refused to believe Jesus was the Christ.

Consider the lesson of Melchizedek In Hebrews 7. The author writes:

For this Melchizedek, king of Salem, priest of the most high God, who met Abraham returning from the slaughter of the kings, and blessed him; To whom also Abraham gave a tenth part of all; first being by interpretation King of righteousness, and after that also King of Salem, which is, King of peace; Without father, without mother, without descent, having neither beginning of days, nor end of life; but made like unto the Son of God; abideth a priest continually. (Heb 7:1-3).

Now, it wouldn't be "white space" to figure out the meaning of Melchizedek's name, his role as king and priest, or even the meaning of Salem. But to realize that he's presented as being without father and mother, and with no end of days, as well as that this is the priesthood of the Messiah, is pure "white space" understanding. It's the spiritual message of Melchizedek found in the white space.

We are blessed to have examples such as these and many others. But the greater blessing is to be given the tools to search out the white space. As Christadelphians, we are dedicated to the truth of God's word. We understand that to uncover the "white space" of the Word of God, it must be read *"from faith to faith."* (Rom 1:17). That is, you must faithfully read the Word (to faith) and understand and accept that it is offered faithfully (from faith). The one who recognizes that the Word of God is holy and true places God's word above their own opinion and prejudices. This task isn't an easy thing to do; our natural inclination is to believe something from our own perspective and seek the Word of God only to reinforce those beliefs. However, reading and believing in His Word from faith to faith is to believe that God is real and His Word is true. When we accept that idea and read His Word *"from faith to faith,"* then the meaning, the principles, and the "white space" of the Almighty's Word are revealed.

The rabbi couldn't see the Second Coming of Christ in Isaiah 53. In fact, in a later video, he denies that Isaiah 53 is even about Messiah, claiming the prophet was speaking about the role of Israel in history. Now, to be fair, you could interpret certain aspects of Isaiah's prophecy as relating to Israel: *"Growing up as a tender plant"* and *"acquainted with grief,"* just to name a couple. But because we know it to be about Israel, the entire prophecy must relate to Israel. Yet, many parts of this prophecy simply can't refer to Israel—not then, not now, not ever. For instance, the prophecy says his appearance was *"not comely"* or impressive, yet Israel is never described that way in Scripture. The nation is repeatedly described as a land *"flowing with milk and honey."* Isaiah 53:9 says he *"made his grave with the wicked, and the rich in his death because he had done no violence, neither was any deceit found in his mouth."* These are words that could never be said about the nation of Israel. Not only do the people have a history of violence (still perpetuated to this day), but their deceitful tongue is constantly condemned in Scripture. Additionally, the soul of Israel never serves as *"an offering for sin,"* (v. 10), not for the nation nor anyone else. That role is relegated solely to Christ, the world's Savior.

In Isaiah 53:9, the Messiah dies. The prophecy reads, *"And he made his grave with the wicked, and with the rich in his death."* It then later says in verse 10 that God shall *"prolong his days."* You don't prolong the days of a dead man. Therefore, the Messiah must die, be raised, and come back. The white space of Isaiah 53 makes it abundantly clear why he had to die, why he would return and what happens when he does. The prophet, therefore, says God, *"Will I divide him a portion with the great, and he shall divide the spoil with the strong; because he hath poured out his soul unto death."* (Isa 53:12).

We are truly blessed to be able to see the "white space" and be transformed thereby. It offers us so much to be reassured and strengthened that we should never take it for granted. By grace, we understand the nature of man, Christ, the atonement, God's glorious plan and purpose, the hope of Israel, the Kingdom to come, and so much more. These truths can transform the mind and renew the heart. So, let's never grow complacent about what we've been given, but give all glory and honor to our heavenly Father, who has chosen to reveal to us the wonder of the "white space."

*Jim Sullivan,
Stoughton Ecclesia, MA*

EXHORTATION AND CONSOLATION

PART 5
PEOPLE WHO KNEW JESUS

By Rick Hill

JESUS says we need to have the faith and trust of a child.

Let the children come to me. Don't stop them! For the Kingdom of God belongs to those who are like these children. I tell you the truth: anyone who doesn't receive the Kingdom of God like a child will never enter it. (Matt 19:14 NLT).

Do our children know Jesus? They do if we have been teaching them and showing them how to live by faith and trust. Jesus also knows our children, and he listens and answers their prayers. We do not specifically know at what age young Samuel was dedicated to God; maybe he was around seven. When did he hear God speaking to him? Possibly in his early teens? We do not know, but God knew him and used Samuel for a specific task. And so He worked with him to prepare him for being a Judge in Israel.

Exhortation and Consolation: People Who Knew Jesus (Part 5)

Here is Gavin's story of faith and trust.

One time, when I was about ten, my dad, brother, and I went to an island on my step-grandfather's boat. We decided to camp there on the island and stay the night. We made s'mores, went fishing, and had a great time until we thought it was time to go to bed around ten o'clock.

We had laid out a few blankets to put our sleeping bags on, along with our pillows. When we walked into the small shack my step-grandfather had built on the island, we were greeted with bugs slightly larger than a cockroach, which we later discovered are called "wood roaches." They were crawling all over the floor. Of course, we were less comfortable staying the night because of their presence. We could do nothing besides brush away the bugs and try to sleep. That did not work! It was around eleven thirty when I decided I couldn't take it anymore, so I went outside and tried fishing, lighting a fire, anything to take my mind off sleeping. Finally, I tried praying. I prayed that the mosquitoes and roaches would go away and that I could sleep and not suffer the night of no sleep any longer.

After that, I thought, "God isn't here. He can't make the bugs just go away." At one o'clock, I went back into the shack and laid down in my sleeping bag, and to my surprise, there were no roaches, and the mosquitoes were gone! For the first time all night, I felt comfortable going to sleep. When I woke up in the morning, I thought to myself, "Why did I doubt God?"

It might have been a small thing compared to death and disease, but I'm still grateful that I know God won't let me down.

A beautiful story of our children who know Jesus and trust God that when they pray, He will answer their prayers.

> *Train up a child in the way he should go; even when he is old he will not depart from it.* (Prov 22:6 ESV).

God has blessed us with our children. God and Jesus love them, and they look after them. Their prayers will be heard.

> *Behold, children are a gift of the LORD, The fruit of the womb is a reward. Like arrows in the hand of a warrior, So are the children of one's youth.* (Psa 127:3-4 NASB).

*Rick Hill,
Picton Ecclesia, ON*

EXHORTATION AND CONSOLATION

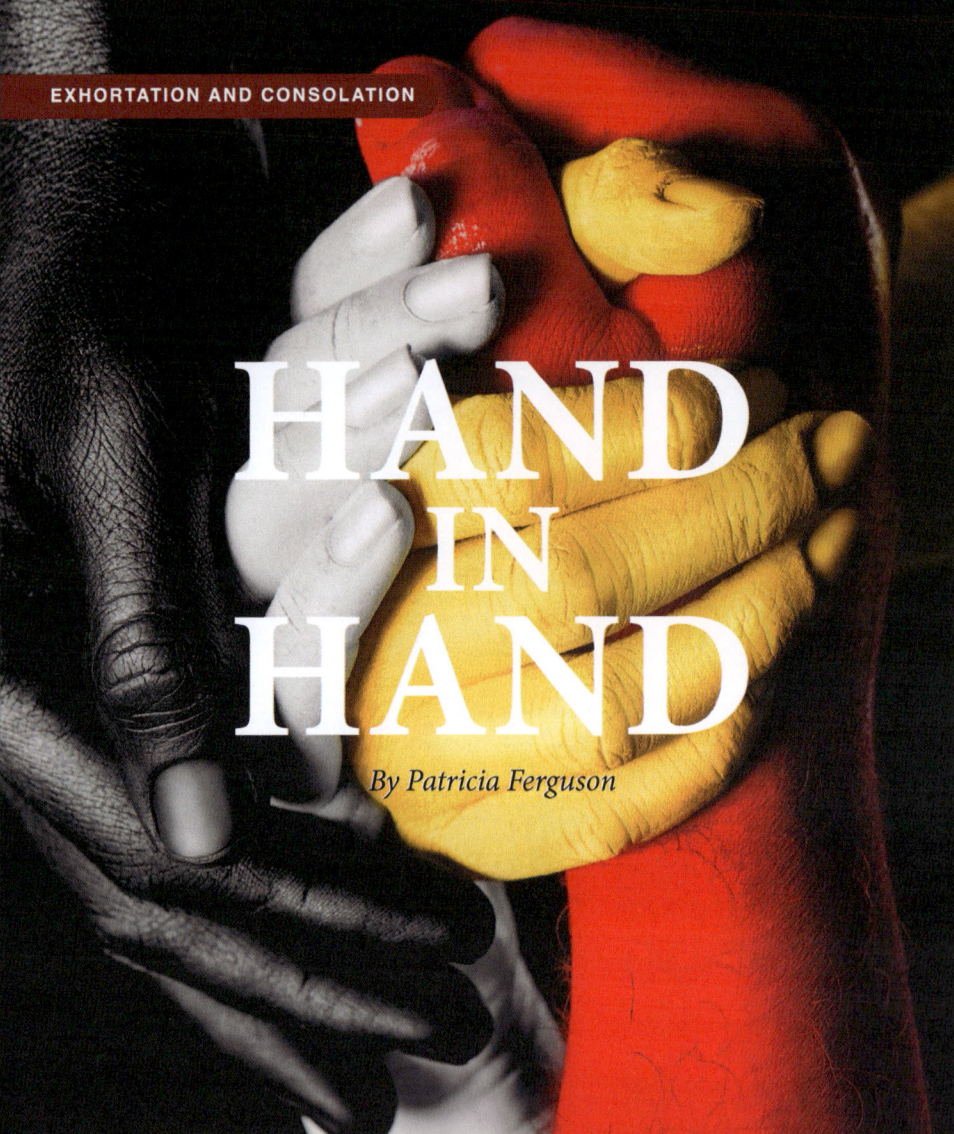

HAND IN HAND

By Patricia Ferguson

OUR mother was a single parent, raising four children under eight. We lived below the poverty line and carried the weight of its humiliation.

When I was nine years old, a family moved next door. Because of their skin color and their son's cognitive issues, they were subject to unfair treatment. No one in the neighborhood would play with their young son. We didn't know why he acted differently, but we were short of playmates and knew Lorne enjoyed hide 'n seek. The rules were simple for him to follow. It was the only time we saw Lorne smile with delight.

We were two households discriminated against for different reasons, but we shared the same end result of feeling insignificant.

Several years later, Lorne and his family moved. Unfortunately, he never received the compassion or assistance he desperately required and deserved. His anger and frustration grew. Sadly, he became a solitary soul and died at a young age.

Do we know children or adults with cognitive limitations? Do we know how being different can impact their understanding of life, who God is, and His message? Each one has their own personality along with particular likes and dislikes. Learning varies from person to person, and individuals' uniqueness can change as they age.

How, then, do we walk hand in hand? As in all things, let's follow Jesus' example to speak clearly and calmly, give praise, exact patience and give a big measure of love. Jesus was patient with the disciples and the multitudes who pressed about Him as they sought his healing power. He took the time to be with little children.

Their belief in the LORD God can help those with cognitive disabilities find peace and contentment. David wrote:

This is my comfort in my affliction: for thy word hath quickened me. (Psa 119:50).

How? By having a sense of belonging in our ecclesial agenda and social structure, giving simple prayers, singing songs of praise, developing friendships, and helping others.

David declared:

And he hath put a new song in my mouth, even praise unto our God: many shall trust in the LORD. (Psa 40:3).

Numerous biblical accounts detail Jesus' investment of time and energy in those excluded by society. (Matt 2:14; John 8:2) Possibly, there were marginalized Jews included in the multitude who crossed the Red Sea and the Jordan. For certainty, marginalized Jews and Gentiles listened to Jesus when he preached in towns, villages and in the holy City of Jerusalem. Jesus and his disciples did not discriminate about who received the message of salvation or their help. It is good to remember God's gift of redemption is present in all places, at all times and to everyone.

> Jesus and his disciples did not discriminate about who received the message of salvation or their help.

And the times of this ignorance God winked at; but now commandeth **all men every where** *to repent: Because he hath appointed a day, in the which he will judge the world in righteousness by that man whom he hath ordained; whereof he hath given assurance* **unto all men,** *in that he hath raised him from the dead.* (Acts 17:30-31).

Patricia Ferguson,
Past member of the now closed Orangeville Ecclesia, ON

BIBLE STUDY

SHOWING FAITH, RELIANCE, AND HUMILITY

LESSONS FROM JESUS' WILDERNESS TESTS

By Tim Jennings

TESTS and trials will always be part of a believer's life. Throughout Scripture, God talks about how He refines us like one purifies metal[1] and will chasten us so we become partakers in His holiness (Heb 12:5-11). We see very little of this process with Jesus. Still, we know he had to learn obedience (Heb 5:8). While his training took place before his ministry began, we do see a final test immediately after his baptism when the Spirit drove him to the wilderness (Matt 4:1-11; Mark 1:12-13; Luke 4:1-14). In these tests, Jesus had to show that he completely relied on God for his needs, that he trusted that God would protect him without demanding proof of that protection and that he had humility. These tests give us an important example to follow as we serve God.

When Jesus was tempted to turn the stones into bread, he responded by saying, *"It is written, Man shall not live by bread alone, but by every word that proceedeth out of the mouth of God."* (Matt 4:3-4). I used to think Jesus was saying that spiritual food was just as important in our lives as physical food. Closer examination shows this statement is about a complete reliance on God. The spiritual nourishment involved in developing and maintaining that reliance means we will trust God to provide everything we need, including food.

This idea is one of the first things Jesus teaches in the Beatitudes. After talking about how God takes care of the animals, he says:

Therefore take no thought, saying, What shall we eat? or, What shall we drink? or Wherewithal shall we be clothed?... for your heavenly Father knoweth that ye have need of all these things. But seek ye first the kingdom of God, and his righteousness; and all these things shall be added unto you. (Matt 6:26-34).

By seeking God first, He will provide us with what we need to survive. By refusing to turn the stones into bread, Jesus showed that he trusted God would provide him with food without abusing the Holy Spirit then and throughout his ministry. We see this happen when the angels minister to Jesus in the wilderness and throughout his entire ministry.

It would have been a legitimate concern for Jesus to wonder how he would be fed and clothed during his ministry. Without a job, buying food and clothes was not an option. How different would his ministry have been if Jesus had to work or beg for his food and clothes?

One way God provided Jesus with his daily bread was through the women who ministered to him (Luke 8:1-3, Mark 15:40-41). There are numerous other examples of Jesus having meals in homes, such as Matthew's feast for Jesus and his friends (Luke 5:29-32).

Jesus knew this reliance on God was something he had to teach his believers. In addition to the Beatitudes, he taught this when the disciples asked how to pray. In the Lord's prayer, he told people to ask God to *"Give us this day our daily bread."* (Matt 6:11). It is reasonable to think Jesus prayed about this every day. Jesus continued to tell the disciples to take no food when they went out to preach because they would be given what they needed (Mark 6:8-13; Luke 9:3-6; 10:1-12). Jesus wanted them to act on their faith. At the end of his ministry, the apostles confirmed they lacked nothing when they preached (Luke 22:35). This example shows that Jesus expects us to rely completely on God in the same way he did. By no means does this mean we should sit back and wait for God to provide for us, but our trust in God should be a fundamental part of how we go about our day-to-day business.

Jesus truly believed that, just as God provided the Israelites with manna, God would provide him with the food he needed during his ministry. How well do we rely on God like this in our life? How often do we let God work through us as He worked through the women who provided for him?

When Jesus was tempted to cast himself off the pinnacle of the temple, he responded by saying, *"Ye shall not tempt the Lord your God"* (Matt 4:7), which is a quote from Deuteronomy 6:16. An important question here is how casting himself off the pinnacle of the temple would tempt God. The full quote is, *"Ye shall not tempt the LORD your God, as ye tempted him in Massah,"* which refers to when the Jews were at Rephidim and demanded water. The underlying issue was that the Jews didn't trust God would provide for them, causing them to make demands of God.

Jesus had good reason to be concerned about his safety since he knew his work would stir up the wrath of the religious leaders of Jewish society because they *"loved the praise of men more than the praise of God."* (John 12:43). Jesus, knowing he would die, had to have known violence would be an ongoing threat during his ministry. There's a certain logic to wanting to see a sign that God would protect him. Because Jesus knew that demanding proof that angels protected him might anger God, and he decided to trust in God rather than tempt Him.

Jesus faced danger throughout his ministry. Before his crucifixion, ten passages in the Gospel records state the Jews wanted to kill Jesus.[2] At one point, the chief priests and Pharisees had a standing order for the Jews to report where Jesus was (John 11:57).

So how do we see Jesus was protected during his ministry? After giving two examples of when the Jews lacked faith, they became so angry they tried to kill Jesus by throwing him off a cliff. The Jews led Jesus to the cliff, putting him in imminent danger (Luke 4:24–29). Jesus escaped by *"passing through the midst of them"* (Luke 4:30). It's important to note that the only action Jesus took was walking through the midst of them. There is no record of Jesus using the Holy Spirit to escape. If Jesus didn't use the Spirit to escape, the only possibility is that the angels protected him, making it possible for Jesus to leave unseen.

This incident is not the only time Jesus escaped death. He hid in the temple to avoid being stoned (John 8:59), and he fled the Jews on two other occasions to evade being killed (John 10:39–40; 11:53–54). In these cases, we see examples of Jesus taking action to dodge danger. He never used the Spirit

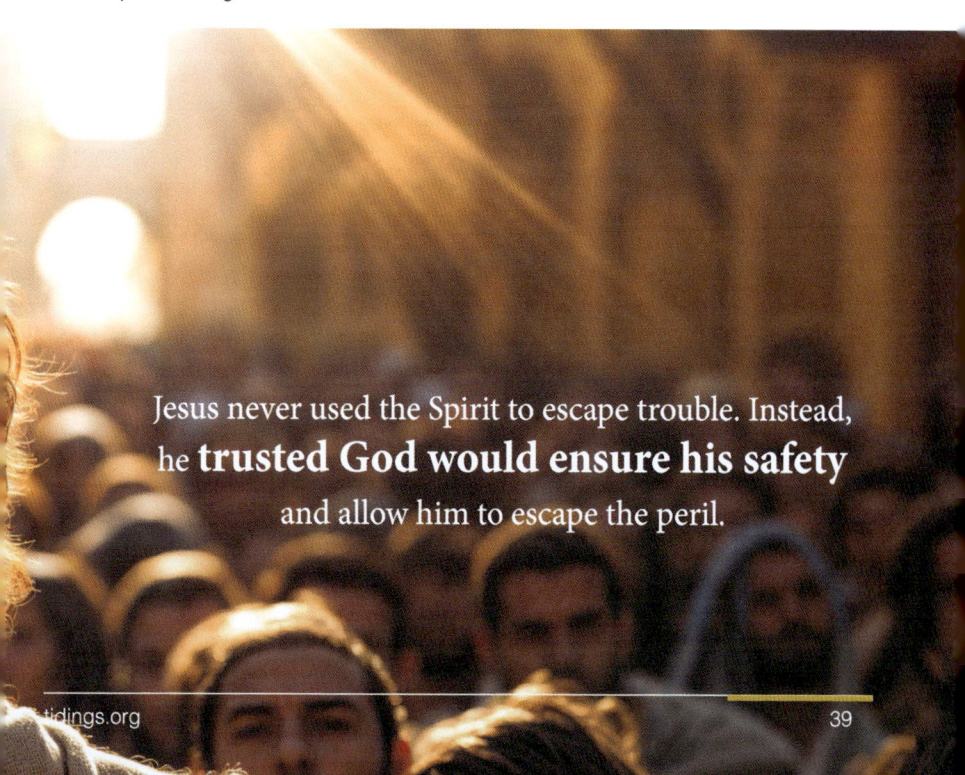

Jesus never used the Spirit to escape trouble. Instead, **he trusted God would ensure his safety** and allow him to escape the peril.

to escape trouble. Instead, he trusted God would ensure his safety and allow him to escape the peril.

In his final test in the wilderness, Jesus' pride was appealed to when he was promised the kingdoms of the world. Rather than exalt himself and claim the kingdoms for himself, Jesus quickly shut down the temptation by saying, *"Get thee hence, Satan: for it is written, Thou shalt worship the Lord thy God, and him only shalt thou serve."* (Matt 4:8-10). Jesus knew, and more importantly accepted, that only God had the authority to exalt people.

Once again, this test of character had a practical purpose. Jesus spent much of his ministry surrounded by crowds who wanted to hear his teachings and be healed.[3] It is easy to see how this kind of attention could feed a person's ego and cause them to think highly of themselves.

In addition to having to deal with the crowds, there were some people who worshiped him.[4] Many people, including his disciples, were astonished by his wisdom, doctrine, and miracles[5] and were amazed by what he said and did.[6] All of this attention caused Jesus' fame to spread throughout Judea.[7]

How quickly would our pride grow if we were so greatly noted for our wisdom and abilities that we were one of the most famous people in the country? A quick look at the world will give us a pretty good idea of what unrestrained pride looks like (though even controlled pride is to be avoided!).

> How quickly would our pride grow if we were so greatly noted for our wisdom and abilities that we were one of the most famous people in the country?

Now imagine what it would be like if people thought you should be king! There are four times in the Gospel records when people talked about Jesus being king: when he met the wise men as a child (Matt 2:2), when he met Nathanael at the beginning of his ministry (John 1:49) when some of the Jews wanted to take him by force and make him king (John 6:15), and when Jesus entered Jerusalem at the end of his ministry (John 12:12-13).

Knowing he was the Son of God, and a descendant of David, taking the kingdoms of the earth must have been a strong temptation. In addition to his "right" to the throne, he could have justified it further by saying he would lead better than the corrupt Jewish leaders and the Romans. With twelve legions of angels at his command (Matt 26:53), his hypothetical military victories would quickly surpass David's. Fortunately, Jesus had the humility required to reject this temptation. By rejecting this temptation in the wilderness, Jesus proved he was ready for the temptations of pride that would repeatedly present themselves during

Bible Study / Showing Faith, Reliance and Humility

his ministry. Before his ministry began, Jesus understood what he explained so clearly to Pilate: that his kingdom is not of this world (John 18:36). He knew the pleasures of this world would last for a short time and focused on the joy God offered (Heb 12:2).

When we go through a tough trial, it is important to think about why we are experiencing it. It could be that God is testing us to see if we are ready for some upcoming work He wants us to do. Or it could be that God wants us to further develop certain traits in our lives. Whatever the reason for the trials and tests in our lives, we must always try to absorb the wisdom God will give us (Prov 2:6; Dan 2:21-22; Eph 1:17) and develop the faith, character, and reliance on God that Jesus showed. The more we become like Jesus, the more we will be filled with God's righteousness. Let us be motivated, like Jesus was, by the joy that God has set before us and always strive toward the Kingdom.

*Tim Jennings,
Verdugo Hills Ecclesia, CA*

---

1 Psa 66:10; Prov 17:3; Isa 1:25; Dan 12:10; Zech 13:9; 1 Pet 1:7.
2 Matt 12:14–15; Mark 3:6; Luke 4:28–30; 6:11; 5:16–18; 7:1, 25; 8:59; 10:39–40; 11:53–54.
3 Matt 4:25; 5:1; 8:1,18; 9:8, 33, 36; 11:7; 12:15; 13:2, 34; 14:13-14, 34-36; 15:10, 29-38; 17:14; 20:29; 21:8; 22:33; 23:1; Mark 3:8, 20, 32; 4:1; 5:31; 7:33; 8:1-2; 9:14; Luke 5:19; 6:17, 19; 8:37; 9:12; 12:1; 18:36; 19:37; 22:6; John 5:3, 13; 6:2.
4 Matt 2:11; 8:2; 9:18; 14:33; 15:25; Mark 5:6; John 9:38.
5 Matt 7:28; 13:54; 22:33; Mark 1:22; 5:42; 6:2; 7:37; 10:24, 26; 11:18; Luke 2:47; 4:32; 5:9; 8:56.
6 Matt 12:23; 19:25; Mark 1:27; 2:12; 6:51; 9:15; 10:32; 14:33; Luke 4:36; 5:26; 9:43.
7 Matt 4:24; 9:26, 31; 14:1; Mark 1:28; Luke 4:14, 37; 5:15.

Whatever the reason for the trials and tests in our lives, we must always try to **absorb the wisdom God will give us** *and develop the faith, character, and reliance on God that Jesus showed.*

BIBLE STUDY

PART 7
WORDS I HOPE I NEVER HEAR AGAIN
By David Levin

Christadelphian Cliches, Misquotes, Pat Phrases, Wrested Scriptures, and Legalistic Formulas

Grace is an Undeserved or Unmerited Favor

THIS month's topic doesn't quite fit the series title. This standard definition of grace is more of an "I hope never to hear it again without it being given due thought as to what it entails." As a fast and easy definition of grace, it doesn't say what it appears to say. There's a simpler and more accurate way of defining "grace."

What's wrong with it? The deficits of the phrase "undeserved favor" are fivefold. First, "undeserved" or "unmerited" (I use "undeserved" in this article, as it is the more comprehensive term) is redundant. Second, the phrase is a negation; it denotes only what grace isn't, not what it is. Third, the qualifier "undeserved" introduces the human element into an attribute that is completely and solely the prerogative of God. Fourth, although Scripture hints at this definition, it's not a Scriptural phrase, probably not for the reasons given here. Fifth, the meaning of "undeserved grace" depends on the meaning of its positive form, "deserved grace." If it turns out that "deserved grace" has no meaning, then "undeserved grace" is in big trouble.

What's at stake? Our understanding of the magnitude and basis of God's grace.

How can it be fixed? The definition is easily fixed by dropping the word "undeserved." Grace is God's favor. That's it, at least for the one aspect of God's grace of concern here. As used in the New Testament, this word has a broader reach.

Discussion: Starting with problem #1 above, the shortest argument to remove "undeserved" is that it's redundant. By definition, "grace" is undeserved, so adding the qualifier "undeserved" makes it like those promotions that offer a "free gift."[1] There's no need to muddy "grace" by qualifying it as "undeserved."

As for problem #2, a definition that is a negation only tells you what something **is not**, not what **it is**. If you see "unpasteurized" on a milk carton, you only know what **didn't** happen to the milk; it was not heated to 130ºF. It may have been rendered safe to drink by another method, but you need more information on the label to know that. Likewise, "undeserved" denotes that grace does not come from our deservedness but does not tell you what might be the basis of the bestowal of grace.

The problem with #3 is that "undeserved" introduces a human factor into God's granting grace. The presence of "undeserved" tracks a hint of self-justification into the pure realm of God's favor. True, it's saying that it's **not** about you, but any human reference, even as a negation (not about you), invokes the awareness of your own merit. It's like that old saw, "Don't think about pink elephants." Or a golfer thinking, "Whatever you do, don't hit it into the trees." You can't think, "Don't hit it into the trees," without thinking—and therefore imagining—hitting it into the trees. Grace is purely God's doing. So adding this qualifier can lead your mind to think, "God's not going to count my… [insert something positive about yourself] because I'm saved by his grace."

tidings.org

43

Problem #4 needs little explanation: "undeserved" grace is not Scriptural coinage. The closest you will find is Ephesians 2:8-9, where Paul could have said it but didn't. Besides the context, there is the conversation about "works of the law versus grace." As explained below, "works" cannot be a basis of "deserved grace" and, therefore, does not help give meaning to "undeserved grace."

Problem #5 requires a lengthy explanation. A negative definition only has meaning insofar as its positive corollary has meaning. That is, "not A" only has meaning when "A" has meaning. In the example used earlier, "unpasteurized milk" means something because "pasteurized milk" has meaning. So what could "deserved favor" mean?

If you're thinking, "Wait—there is no such thing as deserved favor," you're right, of course. If we could do something to deserve God's favor, then it wouldn't be a gift—true. However, that's not the point of discussion. The question being asked here is hypothetical to determine the meaning of "undeserved favor." If there were such a thing as "deserved favor," what would be a logical basis of "deservedness"? Determining what "undeserved favor" denotes turns out to be elusive, but let's look at some possibilities.

Fulfilling Contractual Duties?

To start with, "deserved favor" could not refer to benefits accrued under a system of law. When contrasting the Old Covenant to the New, Paul wrote, *"Now to the one who works, his wages are not counted as a gift, but as his due."* (Rom 4:4 ESV). This means that if you follow these rules, you earn salvation—it's a contract. And if you fulfill a legal contract, you don't **deserve** your payment. You have **earned** it.

For instance, if I hire a contractor to remodel my kitchen, I sign a contract that says he will get paid when he finishes the job. I can't logically say, "You did the specified work, so you deserve to get paid." No, he **must** get paid. Contractual arrangements obviate deservedness, so "deserved favor" cannot refer to our fulfilling any set of duties or performing specified rituals or acts of worship.

Again, please note the intent of the above. It's not about whether we can or cannot be justified by works—we all know where that discussion goes. The point here is to find a basis for the hypothetical construct "deserved favor" that will give meaning to "undeserved favor."

Quid pro quo?

If I do you a solid, you might feel like you owe me a favor in return. There's no legal contract involved, no requirement to return the favor. There's also no **logical** reason to do so. That is, if I do something beneficial for you, you thank me, and that's that. It's something I did for whatever reason or purpose. If you have a "should" moment, that's only an emotional connection, a sense of obligation to do something nice in return.

Regarding God's grace, you can see there's no connection at all. Even if you allow that doing good deeds for others is doing them for God, what is the **logical** reason for this to be a basis of "deserved favor?" God cannot be put in our debt logically, legally, or emotionally. So *quid pro quo* as a basis for deserved favor also falls by the wayside.

A Personal Characteristic?

This category includes personal attributes and personal history. It could be belonging to an underprivileged social class or having had serious health and financial setbacks. People in those categories are often thought of as deserving a good break in life—they deserve special favor to help bring them back to baseline.

While there is an emotional appeal (at a human level) for such persons to receive special favor, there is no **logical** reason for this. This is not to say that God does not look with compassion on any of His creatures, though. It is to say that as a basis to establish a meaning of "deserved favor," personal hardship cannot suffice. If that were the case, then the full definition of grace would be something like: **Even though you deserve grace because of drawing the short straw in life, God does not count that, but bestows grace anyway.** Does that sound even remotely possible?

As I said above, identifying a basis for "deserved grace" is a challenge.

A Characteristic That Makes Sense

There is a personality characteristic that does make a logical choice for the basis of hypothetical "deserved grace:" being the kind of person God would want in His Kingdom. Being the kind of person who would fit well with Jesus the King. We have parallels in our present world: A dispassionate coach looks for players who are the best fit for the team. An employer wants people with the skills and attitudes to benefit the company.

Now we're on to something. If deserved favor is "I've made it my life's objective to be the kind of person God wants in His Kingdom," then "undeserved favor" would have a rational basis. It would look something like this: **You did a fine job of developing the Fruit of the Spirit and living in love, hope, and faith. You have shown yourself to be compassionate, trustworthy, and spiritually focused. You are the kind of person suited for the Kingdom of God. But that won't get you into the Kingdom. It's by my grace alone.**

This thought seems like a basis for deserved favor if there were such a thing. Being the right kind of person for the Kingdom is not a legal contract, nor is it an emotional appeal. It is a logical way to select someone. Therefore, God wants you to be the kind of person who is fit for His Kingdom, but without grace, you're destined for oblivion. Grace is entirely God's initiative and prerogative; spiritual development is your acknowledgment of that fact.

A spiritual life is your response to God's grace, not the cause of God's grace. God has blessed you already with every aspect of grace except eternal life. Our Lord's return brings the completion of grace.

David Levin,
Denver Ecclesia, CO

---

[1] The phrase "free gift" might seem Biblical per Rom 5:15, 16 and 6:23, but it is translated from one Greek word, which otherwise is translated simply as "gift." The addition of "free" perhaps adds emphasis, but that is already implied in "gift."

FIRST PRINCIPLES

THE DEVIL AND SATAN

AN OLD TESTAMENT PERSPECTIVE

By Richard Morgan

WHAT does the Old Testament teach us about the nature of evil, the devil, and Satan? In popular Christianity, Satan is said to be a fallen angel who opposes God, wreaks havoc in the world and is the cause of sin and evil. How do those ideas square with a perusal of Old Testament Scripture? Let's begin with a concordance search of the key terms ***devil*** and ***Satan***. We almost come up empty for *"devil,"* although in the KJV, the plural *"devils"* is found four times, translated from two Hebrew words. Modern versions mainly translate these words by the word *"demons."* We would, however, find the word *diabolos* used in place of Satan and in other passages where Satan does not appear in the manuscript, in about twenty passages in the Septuagint (LXX). We'll come to the LXX later, so for now, let's move on to the word *"Satan."*

Satan

"Satan" occurs twenty-seven times in the Hebrew Old Testament. If *"Satan"* is the name of the agent of evil, according to mainstream Christianity, then we should be able to learn some things about him. However, the very first occurrence of the term presents an immediate problem. That first occurrence is in Num. 22:22, and the Hebrew *satan*—is not used as a name or about an evil angel. In fact, it is an angel of Yahweh who acts as an adversary against Balaam.

In the same chapter, the angel speaks to Balaam and says, "I have come out to oppose (*satan*) you." (v. 32).[1] Therefore, an angel acting on behalf of Yahweh can act as an adversary or satan.

The next six occurrences of Satan are in the books of Samuel and 1 Kings. They all refer to human adversaries. Perhaps a case could be made for saying Satan himself directed these adversaries, but again, the word is not used as a proper noun throughout those passages. It is Yahweh who raises up the adversaries in any case.

If we take the books of the Bible in the common order in most versions, we still haven't come across the fallen angel Satan of mainstream Christianity. However, we **have** come across a lot of sin, evil, and misfortune. Leaving aside Genesis 3 and the serpent, which we will consider next month, think of all the sin and evil described in the Book of Genesis. We have Cain killing Abel, and Joseph sold into slavery, just to give two examples. In neither case do we find any reference to a fallen angel character named Satan or any other malevolent supernatural evil in the context. And that is true for all the sin and evil mentioned in Exodus through to 1 Chronicles 21, where we find the next occurrence of *satan*.

The question needs to be asked: if Satan is such a factor in the sin and evil that plagues our world, why isn't he mentioned? Why doesn't God warn his people constantly about the threat of this fallen angel?

1 Chronicles 21:1 presents us with the first real passage that could be a reference to the mainstream Satan character, *"Then Satan stood against Israel and incited David to number Israel."* That sounds more like it, but when we analyze this passage against the parallel account in 2 Samuel 24, it is a big challenge to the mainstream

tidings.org 47

view. In Samuel, we read, *"Again the anger of the LORD was kindled against Israel, and he incited David against them."* The word **he** cannot refer to an evil Satan character. It must refer to either the anger of God personified or God himself. Either way, the fact that Yahweh is being adversarial to David informs us about the identity of Satan in the Chronicles passage. If we do not take Satan to be God himself in Chronicles, he is at least an instrument of Yahweh, just like the angel in Numbers.

Before turning to the Book of Job, let's look at the final three occurrences of Satan in Psalm 109:6 and Zechariah 3:1-2. In both instances, the Satan acts as a prosecutor. In Psalm 109, God appoints the prosecutor and is paralleled in the verse with *"a wicked man."* The word for *"wicked," ra'*, does not necessarily mean morally evil. It is closer to our English word "bad." In other places, God sends *ra'* angels against Egypt (Psa 78:49) and threatens Israel with *ra'* in Deuteronomy 30:15.

The Satan of Zechariah 3 seems to be more supernatural than the one in Psalm 109. Once again, however, the word Satan is a title rather than a name. He brings the accusation against Joshua, but it is not a false one because Joshua was wearing *"filthy garments"* (v. 3), representing either the state of the priesthood or the nation. Joshua's garments are changed, signaling that God chose to remedy the problem rather than let him be prosecuted. There is no mention of any ill intent for the actions of the Satan in this passage, so we cannot make any conclusions as to his identity. The Theological Dictionary of the New Testament comments:

> A similar picture is given in the fourth vision of Zechariah (3:1-10). Here again we have a heavenly prosecutor, and this time at an actual trial. Here again the *satan* is not an evil power. The accused,

Joshua, is in fact guilty, even though the accusation is quashed. The organ of grace confronts the organ of law.[2]

The main use of the term Satan is in the Book of Job. An important consideration when it comes to Job is its literary genre. Unlike the historical books of the Old Testament, Job is part of the wisdom literature. As such, we cannot read too much into the characters in the book. Job may well have been a historical figure, but the book is written like a thought experiment.[3] The Satan character questions Job's integrity and acts as a prosecutor, just like in Psalm 109 and Zechariah 3. However, it is not so much Job who is on trial in the book, but the retribution principle, which states that the righteous will prosper, and the wicked will suffer. The Satan contends that blessing the righteous does not help them to develop true righteousness. The Satan, however, is proved wrong when Job's blessing is replaced with suffering, and he still retains his integrity.

The main point here is that it is Yahweh, not the Satan, who brings suffering into Job's life. In Job 2:3, God says to the Satan, *"you incited me against him to destroy him without reason."* This is confirmed at the end of the book, where his companions *"showed him sympathy and comforted him for all the evil that the LORD had brought upon him."* (Job 42:11). The word for *"evil"* here is *ra'*.

Following is a summary of all the occurrences of *satan* in the Old Testament:

- Numbers 22:22,32—an angel of Yahweh opposing Balaam.
- 1 Samuel 29:4—the Philistines fear David will be an adversary to them.
- 2 Samuel 19:22—the sons of Zeruiah are adversaries against David.
- 1 Kings 5:4—there were no adversaries at the beginning of Solomon's reign.
- 1 Kings 11:14—Yahweh raised up Hadad as an adversary against Solomon.
- 1 Kings 11:23, 25—God raised up Rezon as an adversary against Solomon.
- 1 Chronicles 21:1—Yahweh moved David to number the people.
- Job—a prosecuting adversary but the evil is of Yahweh.
- Psalm 109:6—a prosecutor.
- Zechariah 3:1-2—a prosecutor.

One theme we can see in many of these passages is that Yahweh raises up a Satan or that Yahweh endorses the actions of the Satan. We can conclude then that the term does not refer to the Satan of mainstream Christian thought.

It is also worthwhile looking at the verb form of *satan*, which is found six times in the Hebrew Bible. Three of those occurrences are in Psalm 109 (see comment on v. 6 above), where David speaks of his enemies who *"In return for my love they accuse (satan) me."* (v. 4). David prays that these accusers may be judged by Yahweh (v. 20, 29). There is every indication David speaks of human adversaries.

The word is also found in Psalm 38:20 and Psalm 71:13. In each case, like Psalm 109, the psalmist complains about human adversaries. The same word is in Zechariah 3:1, where the Satan lives up to his name as he stood at Joshua's right hand *"to accuse him."*

In Ezra 4:6, we read that *"the adversaries of Judah and Benjamin"* (v. 1) *"wrote an accusation"* against them. The word *"accusation"* here is a cognate noun *sitna*. Once again, those providing the accusation are not fallen angels but human beings.

Yahweh Creates Evil

It is useful at this juncture to consider the fact that Yahweh brings *ra'* against people. Unlike the devil of orthodoxy, *ra'* or "evil/badness" is God's purview. A useful passage to consider is Deuteronomy 32:39 which says, *"I kill and I make alive; I wound and I heal."* There is no sense of dualism here. There is not a good god who makes alive and heals and a bad god who kills and wounds; Yahweh is sovereign. The words immediately preceding these in the same verse are a common Old Testament statement about Yahweh—*"See now that I, even I, am he, and there is no god beside me."*

The point is further emphasized by looking at the context. God upbraids Israel because *"they stirred him to jealousy with strange gods"* (v. 16) and *"sacrificed to demons that were no gods, to gods they had never known."*

(v. 17). By saying *"demons that were no gods"* the inspired writer is saying the demons of the nations which Israel went after were impotent; they had no power. In fact, those same demons, to which the nations ascribed the various phenomena of nature are mentioned later, for instance, in verses 23-24. *"And I will heap disasters upon them; I will spend my arrows on them; they shall be wasted with hunger, and devoured by plague and poisonous pestilence."* Things like *"disasters,"* *"arrows,"* *"hunger,"* *"plague,"* and *"pestilence"* were, according to the pagan nations around Israel, demons. For instance, the word translated as *"plague"* is *resep*, the name of a Canaanite demon/deity. However, in this passage, it is Yahweh who is in control of *resep*, and the word, a name in Canaanite mythology, is used for a plague under the control of Yahweh. Yahweh is the one who kills and wounds, not the demons/gods of paganism.

The passage is important because it informs one of the greatest polemics against idolatry in the Old Testament. It is found in the latter half of Isaiah, the so-called Deutero-Isaiah. This book was written to prepare Israel for life in Babylon and Persia, where they would encounter dualistic philosophies like Zoroastrianism. Isaiah preaches that the gods they are to encounter are, as Deuteronomy says, no gods.

> There is not a good god who makes alive and heals and a bad god who kills and wounds; **Yahweh is sovereign.**

First Principles / The Devil and Satan

"I form light and create darkness..."

Isaiah 44 is based on Deuteronomy 32. We know this from its use of the nickname for Israel, *"Jeshurun"* in verse 2—*"O Jacob my servant, Jeshurun who I have chosen."* This name is only found elsewhere in Deuteronomy (32:15, 33:5, 26). Later in the chapter, the prophet Isaiah asks, *"Is there a God besides me? There is no Rock; I know not any."* The word for God here is unusual, *Eloah*, as opposed to the more usual *Elohim*. This passage is the only time Isaiah uses this word, and one of the few times it is found elsewhere is in Deuteronomy 32:15, *"then he forsook God,"* and verse 17, *"to demons that were no gods."* The reference to God being a rock in Isaiah is also a keyword describing Him in Deuteronomy 32.

Why does Isaiah use Deuteronomy 32? Because the prophet wants to remind the people, *"I am the LORD, and there is no other, besides me there is no God,"* (45:5) and *"I form light and create darkness; I make well-being and create calamity; I am the LORD, who does all these things."* (45:7). Just as in Deuteronomy, God doesn't just make alive, he kills or creates "calamity"—*ra'*.

Once again, *ra'* is the purview of Yahweh, not a malevolent fallen angel. The Old Testament is emphatic on this point even as they were about to enter captivity in Babylon, where they would encounter the idea of an evil god.

Diablos

Earlier, I mentioned that the LXX often replaces *satan* with the word *"devil"*—*diabolos,* the same word used in the New Testament. This statement is true for the passage in 1 Chronicles 21, the Book of Job, Psalm 109, and Zechariah 3. However, there are two other uses of the word that aren't in place of *satan*, both found in the Book of Esther. It is worthwhile briefly considering these passages.

tidings.org

51

Esther is one of three books in the LXX that has survived in two distinct Greek manuscripts called **Old Greek** and **Alpha**. Below is an English translation of the **Old Greek** of Esther 7:4, the occasion when Esther tells the king about Haman's plan:

> For we have been sold, I am my people, to be destroyed, to be booty and to be enslaved—we and our children as male and female slaves—and I kept silent. For the slanderer (diabolos) is not worthy of the court of the king.

Who is Esther referring to here? The **Alpha** text, instead of *"the slanderer"* has *"the man who did evil,"* and is obviously referring to Haman. The next couple of verses confirm this when the king asks who this man is, and Esther replies that it is Haman.

There is further confirmation the *diabolos* refers to Haman in the next chapter, which in the LXX reads, *"On that very day king Artaxerxes granted to Esther all that belonged to Haman the slanderer (diabolos)."*

One thing we can learn from this is that the Jews were happy to employ the term *ha diabolos* (the devil) to a human being.

Conclusion

Much of the Old Testament is the story of sinful mankind. And yet, we do not find references in its pages to a malevolent fallen angel tempting people and causing disaster. Why wasn't Satan mentioned in the story of the golden calf? Why doesn't the Book of Proverbs talk about the dangers of falling into the hands of the devil? If Satan is the main foe of mankind, the Old Testament does a terrible job of helping us counter his moves.

It is Yahweh himself who brings *ra'*, evil, bad things, calamity, disaster, into the world, not an evil fallen angel. Even though the Satan of Job is prominent (at least in the first couple of chapters), the book highlights that God brought the suffering into Job's life.

The noun *satan* and its verbal form are most often used for human adversaries. In the few texts where the word *satan* could refer to a heavenly being (1 Chr 21; Job 1-2; Psa 109; Zech 3), there is no evidence it refers to a fallen angel, and indeed, there is better evidence that the satan in each incident is employed by Yahweh or even Yahweh himself as in the case of 1 Chronicles 21.

Next month, we'll expand our reading of the Old Testament by considering the serpent of Genesis 3, a character thought to be either a tool of Satan or the devil himself.

Richard Morgan,
Simi Hills Ecclesia, CA

---

1 All Scriptural citations are taken from the English Standard Version, unless specifically noted.
2 Walton J.H. and Walton J.H. (2019). *Demons and Spirits in Biblical Theology*. Cascade Books. p. 216.
3 Werner Foerster, "Διαβάλλω, Διάβολος," ed. Gerhard Kittel, Geoffrey W. Bromiley, and Gerhard Friedrich, *Theological Dictionary of the New Testament* (Grand Rapids, MI: Eerdmans, 1964–), 74.

HAMILTON, GREENAWAY
ECCLESIA CENTENNIAL

LAST year marked the centennial year that there has been a light stand for the gospel of Jesus Christ at the corner of Greenaway and Wilson in Hamilton, Ontario. Hundreds of brothers and sisters have been members over the years, and well over a hundred of them were baptized in this ecclesia. It is an ecclesia that has seen many transformations.

In August 1871, according to all records, there were twenty brothers and sisters in Hamilton, Ontario. Information is somewhat lacking before that time; however, there is a reference in the *Herald of the Kingdom Age to Come* in the January and November 1856 issues of one brother resident in Hamilton. In 1871, R. T. S. Powell learned the faith and was baptized. His father was described as "a gentleman and pillar in the principal Methodist congregation in the place." Bro. Robert Roberts reported in the *Christadelphian Magazine* (August 1871)[1] that the son, now our Bro. Powell took over his father's business shortly after his baptism. It's important to note the articles in the *Christadelphian Magazine* were very much a preaching tool at that time. Bro. Roberts wrote:

> This young brother has been indefatigable in his efforts to call his neighbours attention to the truth, which his connection with the town, from youth upwards has favoured. He has canvassed his townsmen right and left, to subscribe to the Christadelphian. The result is a list of about 50 subscribers in Hamilton alone. All of these are paying subscribers but

one and are said to express their appreciation of the publication. His plan has been to tell them that he has a paper to which they must subscribe; that he will take no denial; that he will send it to them for a year, and that if they don't like it he will pay it himself, and not trouble them another year; that if they do like it, he will ask them to pay and expect them to become regular subscribers. So far, all but one desired it at the end of the last year to be renewed.[2]

Like many ecclesias, Greenaway has faced its own set of trials over the years. Despite the challenges those trials posed, the light never went out. Many years ago, there was no children's Sunday School. Then a few years later, there was a thriving Sunday School of more than sixty children crowding into a basement. There were curtains as room dividers in an overall space that one would think was crowded if twenty people were in that basement.

Nevertheless, the Sunday School thrived. The children learned the Word of God, and most put on the saving name of Jesus Christ through the waters of baptism. As that generation grew up, most moved away due to jobs elsewhere or marriages to someone further away. Still, the light of God's Word continued to shine on this corner in the center of Hamilton, Ontario. We are quickly becoming an aging ecclesia, having several members in their eighties and even breaking ninety.

The ecclesia today, as some would say, has become somewhat of an ecclesia of refuge. It is an ecclesia strong in faith, grounded in truth, and rich in mercy and love. It is not perfect. I know because I am a member there, and I am far from perfect. We have officially adopted Hymn 427 *(Grant, Lord, Thy Blessing on This Place)* as our ecclesial hymn. I encourage you to read the words to this hymn to know what we are all about.

So, all this brings us to a plea, a challenge. **We need you!**

Maybe you have or will be planning to attend University away from home. Did you know Hamilton is the home of McMaster University, one of the leading schools in Canada? Here is an opportunity to give back to God while you learn.

Perhaps you have been considering going off to the mission field for one or two years? There's a wonderful place to serve right here in your own community. Not everyone is cut out for the extra burden of mission work in a foreign country. There is, however, fertile ground here in downtown Hamilton for those who would be domestic missionaries.

If you have a family, would you consider being a catalyst to restart the children's Sunday School and breathe new life into the Greenaway Ecclesia? Even better, maybe you could encourage two or three other families to join you. What a fantastic opportunity to teach children the real meaning of the truth, sharing, and caring. Whether you are a brother or sister, single or married, with or without a family, you will surely be useful in the Greenaway Ecclesia.

We will let you in on another gem. We mentioned Greenaway is an aging ecclesia, which is true. However, it is not just age in years, but age in years in the faith as well. Oh, the lessons the young could learn from these elders. And what an encouragement the children would be in warming the hearts of our elderly members to see another generation thirsting for the Word of God.

So why Greenaway? The City of Hamilton needs you. They may not all know it, but with your help, more will hear about it. Oh, what amazing things one brother or one family or perhaps two or three could once again do in the downtown of Hamilton, Ontario, at the corner of Greenaway and Wilson.

It's more than keeping alive the 100-year legacy at this location. It is being part of the oil in the lamp so that the light doesn't go out in this small corner of the LORD'S vineyard. As new members, we are certain you will bring new ideas, ideas to spark us all to do more and do better. One more brother or sister or one more family can make a real and lasting difference.

Say not ye, there are yet four months, and then cometh harvest. Behold, I say unto you, lift up your eyes, and look on the fields; for they are white already to harvest. (John 4:35).

If you are willing and able to answer this call, please contact our Ecclesial Sustainability Committee through Bro. Mark Jennings, Recording Brother, markjennings224@gmail.com.

Marilyne Creer,
Hamilton Greenaway Ecclesia, ON

1 *The Christadelphian Magazine*, Issue 86, August 1871.
2 Yes, I also needed to look up the meaning of "indefatigable. It is defined as "always determined and energetic in trying to achieve something and never willing to admit defeat."

Letters to the Editor

IS CHRIST DIVIDED?

We received a number of letters and social media posts in response to the January "Is Christ Divided?" editorial. We have excerpted a few of those received below.

I think people tend to like to live by rules and traditions. This is the beginning of the problem outlined here. Christadelphians began in an era of great sectarian competitiveness. It was a race to be right. For all these years, Christadelphians have concentrated on correctness. We have tried to summarize the God of the Cosmos into a tiny Statement of Faith. It's hardly surprising that this has often failed. Our insistence on correctness is really just another way of living by law.

If our whole focus was where it should be, all of our problems would disappear. Jesus should be the center and soul of our Christian existence—He is the embodiment of God and of God's gift of Grace. Grace has nothing to do with rules or laws. If Jesus was at the center, we would find unity in a shared value. Each of us has personal views of many things within the Christadelphian framework but they simply don't matter so long as our focus is entirely on Jesus.

David Crouch,
Canterbury Ecclesia, Melbourne, VIC

The application of the command of our Lord Jesus Christ to "love one another" should be the first of the first principles for those who seek to be part of the body of Christ.

John Laben,
Richmond-Petersburg Ecclesia, VA

ANNA

I feel the article about Anna gives an incomplete picture, not recognizing the significance of Anna being a prophetess or female prophet.

The text does not support the idea that "prophetess" was a title bestowed on her by other women. There is every reason to believe that Anna was a female prophet in the OT tradition. God chose individual men and women in whom He would place His spirit such that they could speak forth His message. (Num 11:29) *"Moses replied… I wish that all the LORD'S people were prophets and that the LORD would put His spirit on them."* (Jer 1:5,10 NASB). "[God] *have appointed you a prophet."* (Amos 7:16) has a parallelism between prophecy and preaching.

This is what Anna did: *"giving thanks to God and continued to speak of Him to all those who were looking for the redemption of Israel."* (Luke 2:38 NASB).

I would suggest that the description of Simeon, "the Holy Spirit being upon him" fits the definition of a prophet, although Luke does not name him as such. Anna being named a prophetess means she had God's spirit within her, although Luke does not feel the need to say so.

Janet Johnson,
Adelaide Ecclesia, SA

Our Community / Letters to the Editor

AUTHOR RESPONSE: ANNA

I appreciate what Sis. Janet has said, and I believe Anna was a prophetess, just as much as Simeon was a prophet. I certainly did not mean to imply that she was "second class" in any way.

Anna seems to have lived in the Temple, listening to scholars and sometimes joining them in their discussions—at least I "see" it that way. Anna witnessed a wonderful event: the arrival of God's Son carried in the arms of his mother. Anna "saw" in her mind the "sword" that would pierce the soul of Mary. And after Simeon had "departed," Anna went about the business of telling everyone who would listen that she had seen the Lord's *"salvation, a light for revelation to the Gentiles, and the glory of His people Israel."*

"Prophets" and "prophetesses" both see visions of the future and go about teaching their contemporaries.

> *Coming up to them* [that is, Simeon, the baby Jesus, Mary, and Joseph] *at that very moment, she* [Anna] *gave thanks to God and spoke about the child to all who were looking forward to the redemption of Jerusalem.* (Luke 2:38).

And I would venture to say that Anna the prophetess spoke and taught more about the *"redemption"* to come than Simeon was able to convey. In fact, I would say that she was a female "Elisha" to a male "Elijah" after he "departed."

George Booker,
Austin Leander Ecclesia, TX

Please be advised that the San Francisco Ecclesia at Marinwood, CA, has recently changed their name to the **North Bay California Ecclesia.** The recording brother is Bro. Jerry Hirst (yesitsjerrybuilt@gmail.com).

NEW BOOK

One Family, by Bro. Jason Hensley is a scriptural exposition of the relationship between Christians and Jews. It examines the historical context of the New Testament, the literary contexts of various passages dealing with Jews, and the overall Biblical context to demonstrate that the first-century ecclesia saw itself as part of one family with the Jewish community. This book gives the Scriptural backing for the Christadelphian community's actions described in Part of the Family.

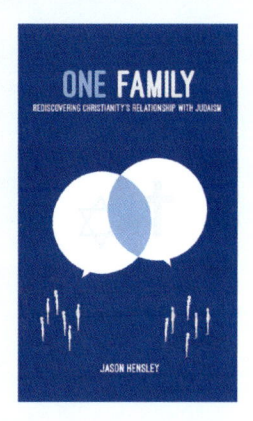

Available from Amazon (link on the *Tidings* Bookstore at tidings.org) or the Christadelphian Library at christadelphianlibrary.com

NOTE

PREACHING AND TEACHING

COSTA RICAN BIBLE SCHOOL

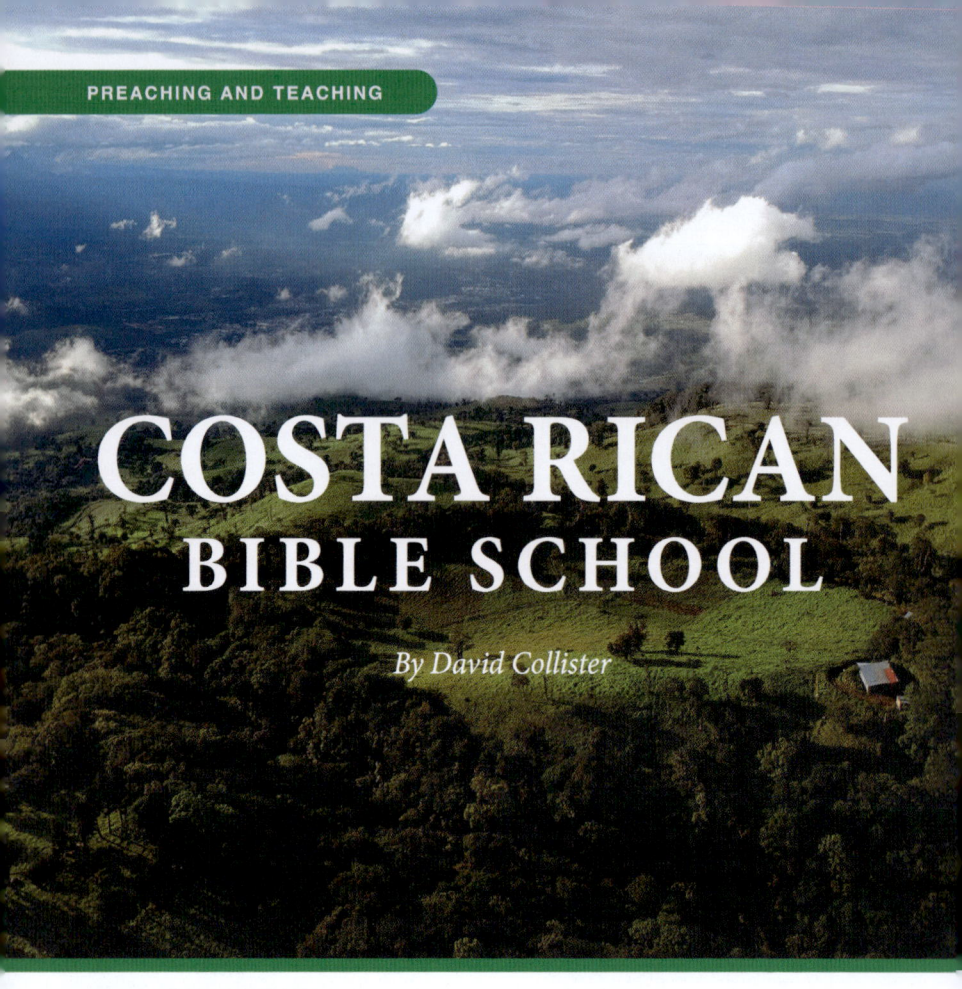

By David Collister

As I have written in previous articles, Costa Ricans are very diligent in their preparations for the year-end Bible School, beginning months in advance to plan out the details. They try to involve as many as possible in the preparations. They always choose a theme for the event and try to tie all the activities into this theme, including the planned free-time activities.

For background, there are two Bible Schools in Central America at the end of each year, one in Costa Rica and one in El Salvador. They are always planned for the last two weekends of the year since many people have holidays over the Christmas and New Year's weekends. Each year, alternatingly, one of the two countries hosts a larger international school, inviting brothers and sisters from neighboring countries to participate. In comparison, the other does a smaller school, mainly for the members of that country. This year, El Salvador was to hold the larger international school over the New Year's weekend. Therefore, Costa Rica held a smaller school just for its own members. Because of this, they decided

Preaching and Teaching / **Costa Rican Bible School**

to rent a smaller locale just outside of Santa Bárbara de Heredia, the town where most of the members live.

The Costa Rican Bible School ran from Friday through Sunday, December 22-24, at the Rancho Los Querubines Sala de Eventos. It is a beautiful venue, with a large meeting room with a kitchen area at one end. The grounds include a large lawn surrounded by beautiful trees and vegetation and a veranda that was used for some of the young people's classes and the brothers' class. Although the locale did not have facilities for sleeping, it was close to town, so it was easy to go back to the houses at night to sleep. This plan worked out quite well and didn't require members to pack. The location was perfect for the size of the group, and the beautiful trees were very apt, considering the theme of the school: "Tejiendo Raices: Juntos Somos un Bosque." — "Weaving Roots: Together we are a forest." It was a clever theme with many spiritual applications and lessons.

This year, as was the case last year, I was asked to prepare and deliver the adult talks, including four main classes and a word of exhortation. As I meditated on how to address the theme, I realized I could broaden it to include not only spiritual lessons on roots and forests but all types of spiritual lessons from trees. It was a fascinating study. I divided the topics into two classes on spiritual lessons from trees themselves, one class on roots, and one class on forests, looking to God's Word for the spiritual significance. My exhortation was to be on the Tree of Life. Satisfied with this division, I delved into the study and learned many amazing facts and lessons from trees that apply effectively to our spiritual lives. Trees are the most mentioned living organisms in the Bible, apart from humans, showing us that God loves trees and has used them to teach us many lessons. Bro. Alex Alfaro gave the teen classes, and Sis. Marisol Araya gave the children's classes. We recorded the classes and made them available online and on Zoom, enabling several brothers and sisters from other countries to join us virtually.

The weekend was well organized, with a schedule each day that included classes, time for fellowship, meals, games, and recreation. The first day began with an Inauguration activity in which Sis. Mariana Ureña gave a short talk about roots and then divided us into three groups to draw a tree and find key verses about trees and roots. The groups presented what they found to the ecclesia. We were each given a bean sprout kit and planted our beans as an object lesson for the weekend. When I left, I decided to leave mine with 9-year-old Isaac, son of Bro. and Sis. Neftali and Zuelen Espinoza, with whom I stayed for the weekend. He's a very friendly and spiritual young man, and I'm sure he is taking good care of it.

Participation from the brothers and sisters was encouraged during the classes. Many good points were shared, which enhanced the classes. We were able to help each other grow in our knowledge and resolve to put the principles we discussed into practice. The exhortation focused on the Tree of Life throughout the Scripture, culminating with the cross of Christ and Christ himself being the Tree of Life. In addition to the main classes, there was also a brothers' class given by Bro. Juan Diego Vargas, and a sisters' class given by Sis. Mariana Ureña.

Another highlight of the weekend was the Teatro Ignis, a series of skits put together by the young people. Topics included our trust in the Lord Jesus and the authenticity of our prayers. The group also did a skit just for fun, which was very amusing. The young people are very talented at acting and always do an interesting presentation each year. Afterward, we all went out to the lawn, where we had a bonfire, snacks, and hot chocolate. At the end, the participants had the opportunity to express what they were thankful for, reflect on the previous year, and look ahead to the coming year.

The weekend ended with a short talk in recognition of all who had participated and contributed to the school, along with a slideshow of the weekend. It was a perfect closing to a wonderful weekend in which we strengthened the bonds of fellowship and reflected on our spiritual lives, helping us to reprioritize and put the things of God first in our lives.

David Collister,
Verdugo Hills Ecclesia, CA
CBMA Link for Costa Rica

PREACHING AND TEACHING

CHRISTADELPHIAN VIDEO

2023 YEAR IN REVIEW

By Art Courtonel

JULY 20, 2023, saw the eleven-year anniversary of the YouTube site and the inception date of "Christadelphianvideo.org".

Through God's grace, in 2023, we provided abundant Scriptural material from across the globe on Christadelphian Video. This material has ranged from "Thought for the Day" videos and daily comments on the daily readings from our WhatsApp group, Bible School and Prophecy Day videos, Gospel videos, Bible classes, and Fraternal videos. This year, we have seen a much larger uptake of shorts/reels since creating our dedicated team headed by Sis. Stef Foley. We have also continued to support ecclesias and other online organizations with their online streaming events.

This year has seen us source, download, produce, review, provide artwork for, and upload over a staggering 2,407 videos. A substantial increase (32%) over last year. We've been more selective this period while producing audio-only versions of each video for our popular podcast Bible.Truth.Feed and Christadelphian Talks.

and another area for our work with the public. We hope to include collaborations with other sites that can help with the follow-up of contacts (e.g., TIYB correspondence courses).

We must thank our review and graphics design teams for their outstanding work in providing reviews and graphics for over 2,400

> **This year has seen us source, download, produce, review, provide artwork for, and upload over a staggering 2,407 videos. A substantial increase (32%) over last year.**

During 2023, we rebranded our "BibleTruthandProphecy" profile to "The Bible Channel—Discover the Bible." This name reflects the content we regularly upload more accurately. We are grateful to all the teams involved with this effort in 2023.

We have not made any progress with our new "Discover the Bible" site yet, but we hope to create something this year, God Willing. if you would like to be involved, please let us know.

Bro. Matt Eggington, our webmaster, has now completed our audio-only site, www.scripturescribe.com, and regularly uploads from his archive material collected over the years, as well as new material converted from video files on our video site. He will continue fine-tuning our Christadelphianvideo.org site while developing our new preaching arm.

The idea behind these changes is to have a resource for the brotherhood

videos during this period. Sis. Beulah Edwards has seen her team grow this year to over thirty brothers and sisters, which has helped to keep the steady stream of new material flowing.

Our graphic designers have been using the exciting emergence of AI (Artificial Intelligence) to create images, and I am sure this resource will be advanced through the coming year.

Our social media presence has grown consistently since 2021 despite our main Instagram account being shut down twice in 2021. It is now renamed www.instagram.com/christadelphian.video. Our preaching Facebook "Bible School" page www.facebook.com/OpenBibles, has proved very popular over the year, now realizing 4,500 followers (+200 over last year). Our events team has been holding two live streams each week on this page via Zoom (Sundays @ 2.30 GMT and

Thursdays @ 6.30 GMT). These live streams have been well received, with some being watched thousands of times.

In addition, our live events onsite team leader, Bro. Luke Brown, along with the help of Bro. Matthew Pearce and Pete Barrett have recorded many events, including the Northern, Rugby, and Young People's Prophecy Days, as well as the Swanwick Bible School and other live events.

We acknowledge the great effort that goes into preparing and recording these events, and the benefit to the community and beyond of having these recordings is invaluable.

We have received donations during 2023 (christadelphianvideo.org/donate) and have funds available to carry out essential work on our network, changing servers and investing in software to ensure the site works much more efficiently than previously. Funds have also been used to promote some carefully selected video material on YouTube, Facebook, and Instagram.

Our main Twitter (now "X") account twitter.com/Christadelph has 1,384 organic followers, the same as last year. We have purchased the "Blue tick" to verify our presence and may well start uploading videos to Twitter for greater exposure on that platform.

We have struggled to upload much content to our podcasts this year due to lack of time, but we have achieved 2.1 M plays and have gained 466 followers on Spotify at anchor.fm/christadelphians-talk.

Every year, we are thankful to the ecclesias that record and make available their studies, Gospel addresses, fraternals, etc., so we can add them to our network for the benefit of all.

Graphics Team

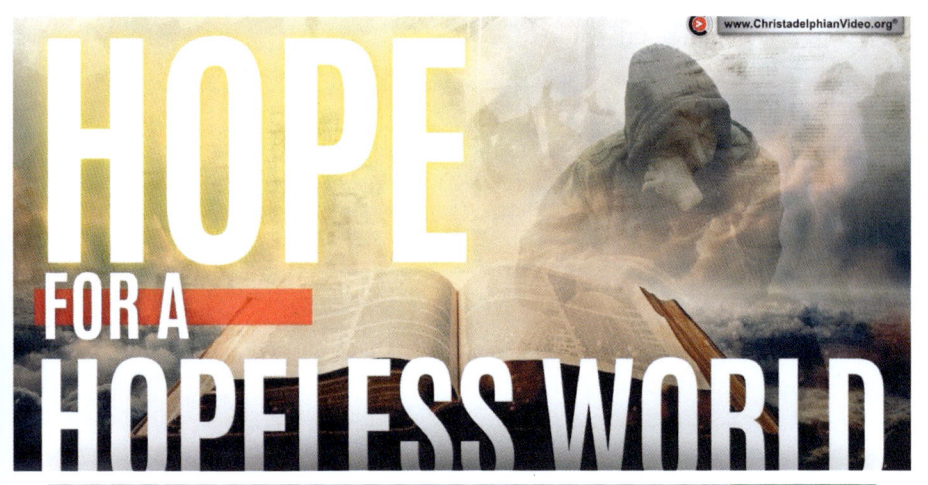

Sis. Gail Williams has done an awesome job coordinating her team this first year. Each day, she provides images for our very popular "Thought" posts based on the readings. She has also identified areas where we could improve our output and communication, avoiding unnecessary work. We are now funding a team Canva account and a subscription to AI image software. I am constantly thrilled by the variety of designs and the imagination used to create such engaging designs by Sis. Gail's team.

Latest Project

In the last year, we welcomed Sis. Stef Foley to our team as team leader/coordinator. Her team concentrated on producing YouTube shorts for upload to Instagram, Facebook, YouTube, etc. These are very popular platforms for these formats, and it is a wonderful opportunity for us to get God's Word to the masses and introduce them to our network. This year, we created 56 shorts/reels—18 of which we promoted with varying degrees of success. Our most watched short was "The Divine Plan: Jesus, Unexpected King Of The Jews," which has had 9,660 views to date. Sis Gail has also been producing some independent shorts created from scratch, and these, too, are great for introducing those interested to the material we offer.

We worked closely with Bre. Frank Abel and Ron Cowie extensively last year to produce many video series specifically for our network and with our audience in mind. We thank them for contributing to this very valuable project and hope to continue preserving and presenting material this coming year with some projects already underway.

In addition to the above, we are now pleased to host a new quarterly publication we both sponsor and endorse—The publication produced by Bro. Nigel Bernard (one of our designers) utilizes the services of various ecclesial members and is called *"Compare and Expound."* Four editions have been released so far, and you can find them at christadelphianvideweeklyument/compare-expound/

Upcoming Events

Sis. Rachael Wadsworth has kindly agreed to manage the Upcoming Events section on our website. We hope this area will grow to be a useful aid for our community as we seek to encourage brothers and sisters to engage with more online and in-person events held throughout the world of Christadelphia. She has long been keen to involve herself in a project like this.

We pray God will continue to use our efforts in His service to bring more people to His saving Grace so that He may be glorified. It is highly possible many individuals have been assisted in their understanding of God's truth via a network that we are unaware of. Certainly, the comments received daily on our YouTube main channel would indicate this.

New Functionality

Sis. Joanna Evans has taken on the role of creating chapter breaks for the majority of all our newly uploaded videos. This update is a rewarding and valuable task to assist viewers of the material find key points within a video, but it is also very time-consuming. She has dedicated herself to this over the last year and has become a very valued member of our network. We thank her for her unwavering dedication to the task.

2024 Plans (God Willing)

We hope to have further collaborations with other online organizations and presenters from within our community.

As our presence grows, we commission more speakers to produce bespoke material specifically for our network, calling on our eleven years of experience and understanding of what works best to attract more to the word of God.

We have also been blessed to receive the services of Bro. Dan Langston, a new videographer, who has been producing the "Bible in the News" consistently each week. These products have always been popular.

In 2024, we hope to continue to support the brotherhood with live events, streaming, and subsequent video editing and hosting.

The year ahead will provide us with many challenges, personally and collectively, I am sure, but it will also allow us to reach out to those seeking God's truth and support our community with sound Bible preaching and study material.

If any brother or sister would like to volunteer within the network in any capacity, please email christadelphianvideo@gmail.com

Art Courtonel,
Rugby Ecclesia, UK
ChristadelphianVideo.com

Thoughts on the Way
Public Prayers

PUBLIC prayers should be relevant. This means they should be related to the immediate purpose, whether an opening prayer, prayer on behalf of others, thanks for bread or wine, etc. For example, there is a time to pray for those who are sick or traveling, but the thanks for the bread or wine is not the time.

Praying in the presence of others may be quite difficult at first for some brothers. There is no problem with a young or inexperienced brother preparing one or more written prayers (suitable to various situations), ready to be used if he is called upon to pray.

Prayers should not be repetitious. There is no need to recount all the key points of the exhortation that preceded the prayer. However, it may be useful to take one point and emphasize that in your prayer. There is no need to pray through the whole plan of salvation just because you can. Keep in mind that young children, never mind their parents, as well as older folks, may have problems with long prayers—either with standing still or concentrating for more than a minute or two.

Prayers should be fresh and spontaneous, if possible. In my opinion, prayers are best when offered in common, everyday language, not old, artificial "Sunday only" speech. Some brothers are well practiced at using King James Version language, and that's fine for them. But young brothers might want to think about praying in the same language they use for common speech. At least it will sound natural and not forced.

Public prayers should be short and to the point. The writer of Ecclesiastes has some useful advice:

> Guard your steps when you go to the house of God... Do not be quick with your mouth, do not be hasty in your heart to utter anything before God. God is in heaven and you are on earth, so let your words be few. (Eccl 5:1, 2).[1]

Jesus criticized the Pharisees because their prayers were carefully crafted to sound pleasing to the listeners and to enhance their own reputations. Here is what Jesus said:

> And when you pray, do not be like the hypocrites, for they love to pray standing in the synagogues and on the street corners to be seen by men... And when you pray, do not keep on babbling like pagans, for they think they will be heard because of their many words. Do not be like them, for your Father knows what you need before you ask him. (Matt 6:5, 7, 8).

Bro. C.C. Walker, a former Editor of *The Christadelphian*, had this to say about what he called "indecorous prayers," that is, inappropriate or unacceptable prayers:

Public prayers should be short and to the point.

The disciples felt their inability so much that they asked the Lord to teach them to pray. And he taught them "the Lord's Prayer." In English it takes only about sixty words. "God is in heaven and thou upon earth; therefore let thy words be few" [Eccl 5:2]. So said Solomon and the "greater than Solomon" (that is, Jesus Christ) upholds it. His own examples are marvels of chaste brevity and simplicity. All acceptable prayer is based upon faith and obedience, coupled with brevity, simplicity and suitability. Thanks for the bread and wine should be carefully confined to the subject. A closing prayer should not epitomize a lecture or exhortation. Prayers that God "will make us" thus and so, without our honest endeavor, are hypocrisy. "The Lord make us truly thankful" is an indecorous prayer. "Father, we thank Thee" is the Christ model.

One final point about prayer. It is more than a tradition for prayers to end with "Amen." This word has a very real purpose. The "Amen" should not only be spoken by the brother praying. It should be echoed by everyone in the audience.

Why is that? "Amen" is the Hebrew word for "truth" or "truly." In other words, an "Amen" after a prayer is a way of saying:

I agree with this prayer. The prayer offered by the brother on my behalf is my prayer, too. By saying, "Amen," I am saying: "Yes, LORD, this is my prayer, too." We are all praying together for what this brother has spoken aloud for us all.

Say the "Amen" at the end of the prayers, and say it like you mean it. If you are not sure you can say "Amen" at the end, it may mean you weren't listening as you should have. And that's a cause for another kind of self-examination: Why wasn't I listening?

One little aside: My grandmother was a devout Christadelphian who grew up in a different era. If the speaker said something with which she wholeheartedly agreed, she would respond with an audible "Amen." At first, when I heard her, I was a bit embarrassed because nobody else was saying "Amen." But after some reflection, I have come to agree with her. Good on you, Grandma!

George Booker,
Austin Leander Ecclesia, TX

1   All Scriptural citations are taken from the New International Version, unless specifically noted.

THE CHRISTADELPHIAN
TIDINGS
OF THE KINGDOM OF GOD

is published monthly, except bimonthly in July-August, by The **Christadelphian Tidings**, 567 Astorian Drive, Simi Valley, CA 93065-5941.

FIRST CLASS POSTAGE PAID at Simi Valley, CA and at additional mailing offices. POSTMASTER: Send address changes to The Christadelphian Tidings, 567 Astorian Dr., Simi Valley, CA 93065.

Christadelphian Tidings Publishing Committee: Alan Markwith (Chairman), Joe Hill, John Bilello, Peter Bilello, Linda Beckerson, Nancy Brinkerhoff, Shawn Moynihan, Kevin Flatley, Jeff Gelineau, William Link, and Ken Sommerville.

Christadelphian Tidings Editorial Committee: Dave Jennings (Editor), Section Editors: Nathan Badger (Life Application), TBA (Exhortation and Consolation), Jessica Gelineau (Music and Praise), Steve Cheetham (Exposition), Richard Morgan (First Principles), Dave Jennings (Teaching and Preaching), Jan Berneau (CBMA/C), George Booker, (Thoughts on the Way, Q&A), John Bilello (Letters to the Editor), Jeff Gelineau (News and Notices, Subscriptions), Melinda Flatley (Writer Recruitment and Final Copy), and Shawn Moynihan (Books).

Subscriptions: The Tidings Magazine is provided **FREE** for any who would like to read it. The Magazine is available in PDF Format online at **tidings.org**. If you would like to order a printed subscription to **The Tidings** you may do so simply by making a donation to cover the printing costs. The suggested donation for printing and shipping to the US is **$70.00;** (we ask for a minimum donation of $50.00.) Foreign countries are higher, see www.tidings.org.

All subscription information is available online at **www.tidings.org**. You may subscribe online and make donations online or by mail to the above address. Information on how to subscribe in other countires is also available online at **www.tidings.org/subscribe**.

The Christadelphian Tidings is published on the 15th of the month for the month following. Items for publication must be received by the 1st of the month. Correspondence to the editor, Dave Jennings at **editor@tidings.org**. Publication of articles does not presume editorial endorsement except on matters of fundamental doctrine as set forth in the BASF. Letters should be sent via email to **letters@tidings.org**. Please include your name, address and phone number. The magazine reserves the right to edit all submissions for length and clarity.

©2024, Tidings Publishing Committee. In the spirit of Christ ask for permission before reproducing any material. Contact us at **editor@tidings.org**

Scripture quotations marked (KJV) are from *The Authorized (King James) Version*. Rights in the Authorized Version in the United Kingdom are vested in the Crown. Reproduced by permission of the Crown's patentee, Cambridge University Press.

Scripture quotations marked (NKJV) are taken from the *New King James Version*®. Copyright © 1982 by Thomas Nelson. Used by permission. All rights reserved.

Scripture quotations marked (NIV) are taken from the *Holy Bible, New International Version*®, NIV®. Copyright © 1973, 1978, 1984, 2011 by Biblica, Inc.™ Used by permission of Zondervan. All rights reserved worldwide. www.zondervan.com. The "NIV" and "New International Version" are trademarks registered in the United States Patent and Trademark Office by Biblica, Inc.™

Scripture quotations marked (ESV) are from the ESV® Bible (*The Holy Bible, English Standard Version*®), copyright© 2001 by Crossway Bibles, a publishing ministry of Good News Publishers. Used by permission. All rights reserved.

Scripture quotations marked (RSV) are from the *Revised Standard Version of the Bible*, copyright © 1946, 1952, and 1971 National Council of the Churches of Christ in the United States of America. Used by permission. All rights reserved worldwide.

Scripture quotations marked (NRSV) are from the *New Revised Standard Version Updated Edition*. Copyright © 2021 National Council of Churches of Christ in the United States of America. Used by permission. All rights reserved worldwide.

Scripture quotations marked (NLT) are taken from the *Holy Bible, New Living Translation*, copyright ©1996, 2004, 2015 by Tyndale House Foundation. Used by permission of Tyndale House Publishers, Carol Stream, Illinois 60188. All rights reserved.

Scripture quotations marked (NASB) are taken from the *New American Standard Bible*®, Copyright © 1960, 1971, 1977, 1995, 2020 by The Lockman Foundation. Used by permission. All rights reserved. lockman.org"

Scripture quotations marked (CSB) have been taken from the *Christian Standard Bible*®, Copyright © 2017 by Holman Bible Publishers. Used by permission. Christian Standard Bible® and CSB® are federally registered trademarks of Holman Bible Publishers.

Printed in Great Britain
by Amazon

COMING SOON

APRIL — THREE THOUSAND SOULS

MAY — MOTHERS IN ISRAEL

To make a donation or to subscribe, visit us at
WWW.TIDINGS.ORG

The brothers and sisters who write for *The Christadelphian Tidings* do so on a voluntary basis, and the magazine is provided FREE to any who would like to read it. The magazine is available in digital formats online at www.tidings.org.

If you would like to order a printed subscription to *The Tidings*, you may do so simply by making a donation to help cover the printing and mailing costs. The suggested donation is US$70.00, and minimum donation is US$35.00. (Check online for rates in other countries.) If you can afford to donate more, please do so in order to help out those that cannot afford to.

The Christadelphian Tidings of the Kingdom of God
First Class Postage paid at Simi Valley, CA
Send address corrections to:
The Christadelphian Tidings
567 Astorian Drive
Simi Valley, CA 93065-5941

Stay connected and up to date. Find us on Facebook, Instagram and Twitter!

ISBN 9798880162628

9798880162628